The Beatles and Film

This concise yet comprehensive study explores the emblematic journey by four young men from Liverpool from the epicentre of teen-led youth culture to the experimentation of the counterculture and beyond.

Beginning with the celebration of Britain's own 'youthquake' in the joyous and genre-shifting *A Hard Day's Night* (1964), the author delves into how the Beatles' film work allows us to chart their subsequent musical maturation and retreat from the tribulations of stardom in *Help!*, their tentative attempts at improvised filming in the televised *Magical Mystery Tour* (1967), their acceptance of cartoon representations as leaders of the hippie counterculture in *Yellow Submarine* (1968), and the final implosion of their musical dynamic in the recording studios of *Let It Be* (1970). The book analyses how, as they grow with their fanbase, the Beatles' films alternate stylistically between mimetic representation and allegorical interpretation, and switch narratively between fan-filled and welcoming worlds, to films relaying introspection and isolation.

Offering an in-depth case study of the successes and failures of British youth culture in a volatile decade, *The Beatles and Film* is an engaging text for both scholars and general readers alike.

Stephen Glynn lectures in Film and Television at De Montfort University. His research specialisms are in British film genres and the interconnections between film and popular music. Previous monographs on cinema and youth culture range from the general, *The British Pop Music Film* (London: Palgrave Macmillan, 2013), to the specific, *A Hard Day's Night* (London: IB Tauris, 2005) and *Quadrophenia* (London and New York: Wallflower, 2014).

Cinema and Youth Cultures

Cinema and Youth Cultures engages with well-known youth films from American cinema as well the cinemas of other countries. Using a variety of methodological and critical approaches the series volumes provide informed accounts of how young people have been represented in film, while also exploring the ways in which young people engage with films made for and about them. In doing this, the Cinema and Youth Cultures series contributes to important and long-standing debates about youth cultures, how these are mobilized and articulated in influential film texts and the impact that these texts have had on popular culture at large.

Series Editors: Siân Lincoln and Yannis Tzioumakis

Y Tu Mamá También
Mythologies of Youth
Scott L. Baugh

Halloween
Youth Cinema and the Horrors of Growing Up
Mark Bernard

American Pie
The Anatomy of Vulgar Teen Comedy
Bill Osgerby

Bande de Filles
Girlhood Identities in Contemporary France
Frances Smith

Gidget
Origins of a Teen Girl Transmedia Franchise
Pamela Robertson Wojcik

The Beatles and Film
From Youth Culture to Counterculture
Stephen Glynn

For more information about this series, please visit: https://www.routledge.com/Cinema-and-Youth-Cultures/book-series/CYC

The Beatles and Film
From Youth Culture to Counterculture

Stephen Glynn

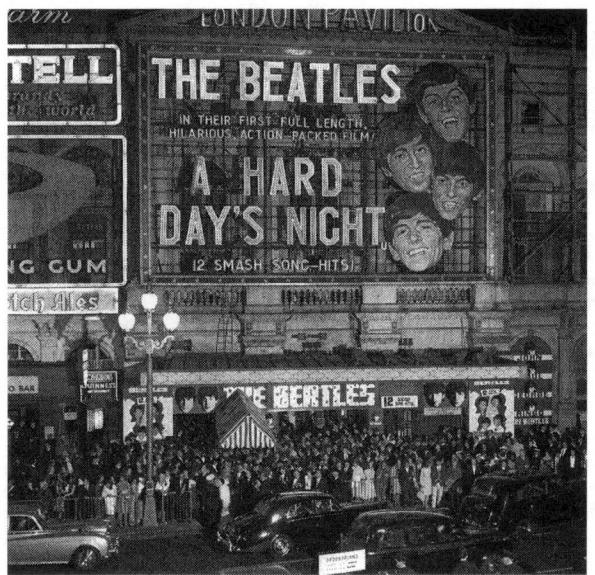

Routledge
Taylor & Francis Group

LONDON AND NEW YORK

First published 2021
by Routledge
2 Park Square, Milton Park, Abingdon, Oxon OX14 4RN

and by Routledge
52 Vanderbilt Avenue, New York, NY 10017

Routledge is an imprint of the Taylor & Francis Group, an informa business

British Library Cataloguing-in-Publication Data
A catalogue record for this book is available from the British Library

Library of Congress Cataloging-in-Publication Data
Names: Glynn, Stephen, author.
Title: The Beatles and film: from youth culture to counterculture/ Stephen Glynn.
Description: London; New York: Routledge, 2021. |
Series: Cinema and youth cultures | Includes bibliographical references and index. |
Identifiers: LCCN 2020026026 | ISBN 9780367225278 (hardback) | ISBN 9780429275357 (ebook)
Subjects: LCSH: Beatles–In motion pictures. | Beatles–Influence. | Motion pictures and rock music. | Popular culture–History–20th century.
Classification: LCC ML421.B4 G59 2021 | DDC 782.42166092/2–dc23
LC record available at https://lccn.loc.gov/2020026026

ISBN: 9780367225278 (hbk)
ISBN: 9780429275357 (ebk)

Typeset in Times New Roman
by Deanta Global Publishing Services, Chennai, India

Contents

Figures

Series editors' introduction

Despite the high visibility of youth films in the global media marketplace, especially since the 1980s when Conglomerate Hollywood realised that such films were not only strong box office performers but also the starting point for ancillary sales in other media markets as well as for franchise building, academic studies focusing specifically on such films were slow to materialise. Arguably the most important factor behind academia's reluctance to engage with youth films was a (then) widespread perception within the Film and Media Studies communities that such films held little cultural value and significance, and therefore were not worthy of serious scholarly research and examination. Just like the young subjects they represented, whose interests and cultural practices have been routinely deemed transitional and transitory, so were the films that represented them perceived as fleeting and easily digestible, destined to be forgotten quickly, as soon as the next youth film arrived in cinema screens a week later.

Under these circumstances, and despite a small number of pioneering studies in the 1980s and early 1990s, the field of 'youth film studies' did not really start blossoming and attracting significant scholarly attention until the 2000s and in combination with similar developments in cognate areas such as 'girl studies.' However, because of the paucity of material in the previous decades, the majority of these new studies in the 2000s focused primarily on charting the field and therefore steered clear of long, in-depth examinations of youth films, or were exemplified by edited collections that chose particular films to highlight certain issues to the detriment of others. In other words, despite providing often wonderfully rich accounts of youth cultures as these have been captured by key films, these studies could not have possibly dedicated sufficient space to engage with more than just a few key aspects of youth films.

In more recent (post-2010) years a number of academic studies have started delimiting their focus and therefore providing more space for in-depth examinations of key types of youth films, such as slasher films and biker films or examining youth films in particular historical periods. From that point on, it was only a matter of time before the first publications that focused exclusively on key youth films from a number of perspectives appeared (*Mamma Mia! The Movie*, *Twilight* and *Dirty Dancing* were among the first films to receive this treatment). Conceived primarily as edited collections, these studies provided a multifaceted analysis of these films, focusing on such issues as the politics of representing youth, the stylistic and narrative choices that characterise these films and the extent to which they are representative of a youth cinema, the ways these films address their audiences, the ways youth audiences engage with these films, the films' industrial location and other relevant issues.

It is within this increasingly maturing and expanding academic environment that the **Cinema and Youth Cultures** volumes arrive, aiming to consolidate existing knowledge, provide new perspectives, apply innovative methodological approaches, offer sustained and in-depth analyses of key films and therefore become the 'go-to' resource for students and scholars interested in theoretically informed, authoritative accounts of youth cultures in film. As editors, we have tried to be as inclusive as possible in our selection of key examples of youth films by commissioning volumes on films that span the history of cinema, including the silent film era; that portray contemporary youth cultures as well as ones associated with particular historical periods; that represent examples of mainstream and independent cinema; that originate in American cinema and the cinemas of other nations; that attracted significant critical attention and commercial success during their initial release and that were 'rediscovered' after an unpromising initial critical reception. Together these volumes are going to advance youth film studies while also being able to offer extremely detailed examinations of films that are now considered significant contributions to cinema and our cultural life more broadly.

We hope readers will enjoy the series.

Siân Lincoln and Yannis Tzioumakis
Cinema and Youth Cultures Series Editors

Acknowledgements

In my life it all began with the Beatles, a childhood Christmas viewing of *A Hard Day's Night* shaping my love of cinema and youth culture: this volume acknowledges the group's seminal influence. My thanks also to another 'Fab Four': to the Routledge series editors, Siân Lincoln and Yannis Tzioumakis, for their advice in helping this volume come together; and to Sarah and Roz, as ever the recipients of all my loving.

Introduction
Overviews and origins

Interviewed in 2012, America's pantheon director Martin Scorsese eulogised over what he termed 'one of my favourite moments in movies', a moment that 'influenced a lot of the work I've done'. After contextualising how overall 'The freedom of the picture was something that was very important: the sense of breaking all the form', Scorsese moved onto his chosen scene where, he emphasised, there was 'something very musical and dancelike about the editing', while the filming possessed a creative tension with 'the freedom of the camera alongside the constraint of the characters looking towards the lens' (quoted in *Arena* ... 2012). One of most cine-literate of directors and a recognised champion of world film history and preservation, Scorsese was not highlighting the skills of his idolised Michael Powell, nor the work of other revered filmmakers such as John Ford, Jean Renoir, Stanley Kubrick, or Alfred Hitchcock. No: his praise here was reserved for the title-track sequence to a television film of 1967, a debut-directed and long-derided piece largely improvised and under an hour in length, a work so neglected that reputedly no negative had been properly archived – Scorsese was lauding Apple Corps' production of the Beatles' *Magical Mystery Tour*. Though pilloried at the time of its release, the film has of late been restored, re-released and reappraised – with the help of authorities like Scorsese – as a seminal example of a key aspect in the work of the most important pop group in western culture – the Beatles and their films.

The Beatles' treatment by academia now constitutes a long and winding road, with myriad volumes dedicated to assessing their lasting influence from musicological, industrial, linguistic, sociological and cultural perspectives (see Inglis 2013). One of that long road's less excavated sections, however, concerns their film work, the focus of this volume. Throughout their career, the Fab Four made regular recourse to film, be it as corporate exploitation or a vehicle for personal expression. Beat poet Allen Ginsberg saw the Beatles' progression from mop-top heart-throbs to disciples of transcendental meditation as constituting 'a "paradigm for the whole era", symptomatic of the whole cultural change the sixties ushered in' (Taylor 1987: 137), and this volume aims to demonstrate how the films of the Beatles offer a prism through which one can trace these seismic youth movements of the 1960s. It explores this emblematic celluloid journey by four young men from Liverpool from the epicentre of teen-led youth culture to the mind-expanding experimentation of the counterculture and beyond. Enacting a fluctuating synergy as they grew with their fanbase, *The Beatles and Film* charts both the successes and failures of youth culture, British and beyond, in a varied and volatile decade.

Firstly, some broad-stroke parameters must be drawn. It is a given that the primary importance of the Beatles' films was understood to reside in their music, and the very acceptance of the Beatles into cinema can be interpreted as contributing as much to the pop music industry as to the film industry. Indeed, the narrative content of the majority of these films could be read as largely 'incidental' to the songs and performance sequences. Music is central to myriad subcultures, and this study acknowledges and explores the importance of the Beatles' musical sequences, but there already exist studies that have concentrated on discrete and detailed analyses of how the Beatles' musical numbers function both intratextually, within their discrete film setting (Fremaux 2018), and intertextually, within the broader scope of the filmed musical genre (Glynn 2013). The principal focus of this study, therefore, is on the Beatles' film work as an attitudinal indicator of youth socio-cultural movements. From the outset this is distinctive. If the development of young people's identities and personhood is generally recognised as a social activity undertaken via sustained interaction with significant others, the Beatles' films begin by showing a precocious advance on early top-down models of socialisation whereby responsible adults (notably parents and teachers) are acknowledged as transmitting stable cultural norms and knowledge by inculcating long-established social attitudes and practices. Here from the outset is the dynamic engagement by Beatles fans in an emergent adult-free socio-cultural framework allowing the interactive realisation of their sense of selfhood.

The terminology at work here also needs addressing. In this study 'youth' is understood as conveying a wider significance than 'teenage', especially as 'teen films' have tended to emphasise experiences of and in (predominantly US) high school. The Beatles and their fanbase extend beyond this focus to a number of identity factors, both post- and pre-adolescence, including the 'elongation' of youth – the exploration of lifestyles deferring traditional milestones of maturation such as settling down, starting a family, etc. These permeable temporal parameters encompass the differing youth cultures on show in the Beatles' films. Their early films, *A Hard Day's Night* (Lester, 1964) and *Help!* (Lester, 1965), are examples and examinations of the strand of youth culture commonly labelled Beatlemania, a commercially exploitative campaign centred on four trendsetting young men that nonetheless elides with a resistant, sexually defiant subculture shaped by its female teen and pre-teen audience. The group's middle films, *Magical Mystery Tour* (the Beatles, 1967) and *Yellow Submarine* (Dunning, 1968), offer more consciously artistic explorations of late-1960s counterculture, a youth movement commonly equated with hippiedom. This phase can, perhaps counter-intuitively, be adjudged as ultimately less 'revolutionary' than Beatlemania. Firstly, the Beatles arguably function here more as adaptors, even followers, than founders or frontrunners. Secondly, they eschew what Raymond Williams terms the more 'oppositional' stance of US and European counterculture which 'finds a different way to live and wants to change the society in its light'; instead they work within the UK's 'alternative' version that 'simply finds a different way to live and wishes to be left alone with it' (2005 [1980]: 41–2). Self-penned or otherwise, the Beatles' counterculture films reveal a fixation less on societal and political change than on attitudinal and personal development. This introspective element continues into their final film, *Let It Be* (Lindsay-Hogg, 1970), which shows the Beatles, and youth culture in general, of an age to reminisce, revisit roots, and mine what can be termed another 'alternative' or 'youth heritage'.

Finally, while 'cinema' is regularly referenced as a medium (and presently as a physical performance space), this book has specifically employed 'film' in its title since it analyses and references not only theatrically-released works by and/or about the Beatles but also television broadcasts and underground/avant-garde exhibited events. Thus, to clarify a difference of scope as well as nomenclature, by privileging an extended period of film production this study differs from current companion volumes in the Routledge Cinema and Youth Cultures series in not centring its study on a single youth film. Instead, in the following chapters, its examination considers all five films starring the Beatles from 1964 to 1970, elaborating how together they offer a heuristic vehicle for tracking the development of youth culture and counterculture across the 1960s.

This study of the five films by the Fab Four offers a tripartite investigation, explaining the motivations and manoeuvrings of their production histories, summarising their critical and commercial reception, and analysing the film 'texts' themselves. The last element constitutes the main body of each section and looks to place the visual style and narrative ideology in its social context, exploring how youth cultures are mobilised and articulated, and the impact of such texts on popular culture at large. The films, of course, are never simply reflectionist, but select from, mediate and at times – such was the group's influence – even trigger social and cultural change. The Beatles on screen are shown to offer a 're-presentation' or a 'refracted' view of the 1960s, their star status giving them a synecdochic function, rendering them a repository for the culture's shifting tendencies and tensions – exemplars of what Christine Gledhill terms 'condensers of moral, social and ideological values' (1991: 215). By dint of their talent, fame and fortune, the Beatles are, of course, not 'typical' members of society, but their films nonetheless articulate the same social aspirations enjoyed and the strictures endured by many of their non-famous and younger followers. While the Beatles' early songs stressed the positives of life and love, harmoniously/ inclusively proclaiming 'yeah, yeah, yeah', their touring workload and public scrutiny rapidly intensified and amplified their physical and psychical confinement. This study explores how their five films trace this oscillating rapport between the Beatles and their fanbase. It shows how the films play out a repeated pattern that alternates stylistically between mimetic representation and allegorical interpretation, and that switches narratively between worlds that are fan-filled and welcoming to scenarios that relay group introspection and even isolation. It demonstrates how their films advocate then retreat from first youth culture, then counterculture, and finally reject the entire cultural construct known as 'Beatles'.

This pattern of acceptance and rejection is initially enacted in the two Beatles films directed by Richard Lester. Following this introductory chapter's explanation of methodology and a brief socio-cultural context for their early and formative relationship with cinema, Chapter 1 analyses *A Hard Day's Night*, arguably the most aesthetically achieved of all pop music films. I have written extensively elsewhere on the Beatles' debut feature, but that earlier monograph, while giving some attention to youth cultures, focuses particularly on the film's contribution to genre development and an understanding of national identities (Glynn 2005). Here, the focus is on Lester's ironised drama-documentary format which (ostensibly) allows the viewer privileged testimony to the epicentre of this new youth culture phenomenon but simultaneously reveals the extent to which the Beatles are already marketed and mediated. It also shows how the film investigates the nature of the fanbase feeding into the unparalleled mass hysteria of Beatlemania.

The series to which this volume contributes aims to explore how young people engage with the culture made for and about them and so, above all, the study of *A Hard Day's Night* examines those (predominantly but not exclusively) female fans. Accounts of youth cultures have long been accused of displaying a gender imbalance by focusing on mainly working-class but overwhelmingly male subjects (McRobbie 1980: 37–49). Lester's film, however, arguably the first concerted examination of the synergy between fans and youth culture, offers a different and distaff perspective. It works to place its young audience centre screen and suggests how, in their chase and concert sequences, the female fans are not merely socialised into a subservient and idolising gender role, but more pro-actively assert a newly-found collective and even transgressive power. In summary, *A Hard Day's Night* is shown as evidencing the Beatles and their youth culture fanbase in mutual (and climactically euphoric) acceptance.

Nonetheless, the Beatles' film debut was not without intimations that this partnership was troubled by more claustrophobic aspects. Chapter 2, examining their sophomore offering *Help!*, explores how, through a more consistent process of displacement, this 'downside' to Beatlemania is given fuller rein. As evident from the lyrical content of the title song, the group are seen as adrift, recipients of unprecedented success but unsure it has been worth the effort. Indeed, amidst the film's elaborate and intertextual espionage plot parodies, the Beatles become marginalised in their own production. Further still, the fans, so integral to *A Hard Day's Night* and its euphoria, are shown here to be excised. Instead, the chapter argues, these fans are allegorised, with the pursuit of the Beatles by a band of Eastern cultists and the constant interruptions to their performances symbolically playing out the group's besieging by indiscriminate and inattentive followers. In summary, we witness in *Help!* the Beatles' (coded) rejection of their youth fanbase.

Help! promotes a new youth cultural imperialism whilst also evidencing the Beatles' retreat from public performance in favour of studio production, an indication of their growing musical seriousness and complexity. Chapter 3 follows how this maturation continued in their changing physical image and the self-filmed, Scorsese-admired *Magical Mystery Tour*, a work furthering their rejection of 'the desire to be seen as the establishment's role model for youth' (Neaverson 1997: 67) but also showing their new attempts to re-position themselves as authentic 'artists and counterculturalists' (Frontani 2007: 16). Challenging the production and exhibition processes of mainstream film-making, the loose narrative resituating of West Coast hippiedom into a British seaside day trip is shown as seeking to replicate, especially in its musical numbers, both the perception-altering experience of an LSD-induced psychedelic trip and the bliss of India-originating transcendental meditation. Analysis of the work's reception reveals, however, that this was the wrong medium at the wrong moment and constituted the first popular and critical artistic failure of the group's career. Here, in summary, were the Beatles once more reaching out to their fanbase, but that fanbase now rejecting the Beatles and their version of the counterculture.

Not for long, though. The bulk of Chapter 3 shows how the group's cinematic fortunes would soon reverse in a project to which they made little personal commitment, but where the use of their personae and the more flexible format of animation allowed a more fully 'realised' version of psychedelia and the concerns of counterculture – the musical fantasy *Yellow Submarine*. A detailed visual analysis shows the myriad artistic influences on the film, notably styles and imagery taken from pop artists ranging from Peter Blake to Andy Warhol. The textual analysis offers potential interpretations for the film's narrative, including its (again allegorical) play on late-1960s states of consciousness and statesmanship: as Bob Neaverson describes it, 'an underground parable of how the psychedelic Beatles (symbols of the peaceful and apolitical forces of hippy counter-culture) overcome the forces of state power to establish a new regime of karmic awareness and universal goodwill' (1997: 88). Accessible at different levels of interpretation, the film's healthy commercial returns would support the reading that, in summary, *Yellow Submarine* allowed their fanbase a delayed (and diluted) acceptance of the Beatles and their (cartoon) brand of counterculture.

The last chapter provides a summative conclusion on how the Beatles and their films re-present the development of (primarily British) youth culture throughout the 1960s. (And beyond: a final survey of their solo film ventures notes how, if the musical core rests with Lennon and McCartney, the film kudos goes to Starr and Harrison). The chapter begins with an exploration of their final film, *Let It Be*, its record of the group's bitter dissolution presenting a parallel to the fragmentation of pop and youth culture at the end of the decade. Containing a compendium of Beatles film tropes, its filmed studio sessions are shown to offer less stylised versions of the musicianship foregrounded in *Help!*. They culminate, however, in one last meaningful live performance, a link back to the group's film origins in *A Hard Day's Night* – until the *Yellow Submarine*-style 'blue meanies' from the British police force close it down. With this volume's focus on 'the Beatles growing up', several factors – notably fan pressure – are seen as contributing to their fractious demise, but *Let It Be* exposes internal splits and new romantic, distinctly adult alliances, which signal unmistakably the end of the youth cultural and cinematic journey. Here, in summary, is where the Beatles reject the Beatles.

In *Let It Be* the Beatles even move out of Twickenham Film Studios, dissatisfied with its atmosphere and acoustics. How different this rejection of venue was to the group's origins where music and cinema worked symbiotically. Prior to *A Hard Day's Night*, the burgeoning Beatles gained plentiful experience, not of film-making, but of cinema houses. It is accepted that the group tightened its act in the bars of Hamburg (Gladwell 2008: 35–68; Inglis 2012), a residency where for the first four months their cramped accommodation was in the Bambi Kino picture house. But on returning to Britain their sound – and name – were predominantly spread by their manager Brian Epstein who had them join the bill of one of the numerous six-act, twenty-minutes-a-set, twice-nightly line-ups that relentlessly toured the nation's cinemas (and occasional ballrooms) in the early 1960s. With most towns' theatres committed to hosting week-long variety acts, these single-booked 'two house' package tours became a welcome source of revenue for

Britain's then-struggling cinema chains. Many of their imposing art-deco-style picture houses, built during the interwar boom years, could seat up to 3000 paying customers and had been fitted with large stages, and even orchestra pits, to accommodate the vogue for cine-variety, a 'bastard form' where film projection was mixed with older forms of popular entertainment (Sutton 2000: 46–7). Suddenly re-theatricalised after years of sharp audience decline, these cinemas now became the prime venue for bringing the freshest pop music acts into a city's High Street.

So it was with the Beatles. Following their modest debut hit with 'Love Me Do', the Beatles' first UK tour, from 2 February to 3 March 1963, had ten of its 14 dates at cinema venues. Beginning at the Gaumont Cinema, Bradford, and taking in the UK's main chains – nights quickly followed at Bedford's Granada Cinema, Wakefield's Regal, Carlisle's ABC and the Southport Odeon – the Beatles started by closing the first half of each 'house', a support act down a bill compered by Irish comedian Dave Allen and headed by 16-year-old Helen Shapiro (Lewisohn 1992: 98–102). Shapiro was a genuine pop music film star who had taken a lead role in Richard Lester's *It's Trad, Dad!* aka *Ring-a-Ding Rhythm* (1962), and performed two songs in the Billy Fury vehicle *Play It Cool* (Winner, 1962) (see Figure 0.1). Nonetheless, the February chart-topping success of 'Please

Figure 0.1. 'Love Me Do': the Beatles' cinematic beginnings.

Please Me' saw the Beatles end the tour as the main attraction, accompanied by a steady growth in screaming from the now packed-out predominantly teenage audiences. This surfacing of what the national press would six months later term Beatlemania was a phenomenon essentially fostered in Britain's cinemas. At Epstein's insistence, the Beatles almost immediately undertook a second tour, their 9–31 March schedule comprising 21 dates of which 13, starting at the East Ham Granada, were again cinema-based (Lewisohn 1992: 103–5). Though nominally now sharing top billing, American singers Tommy Roe and Chris Montez were immediately usurped by the rapturously received emergent teen idols.

These package tours were high-pressured and low-comfort affairs – their drudgery is lightly touched on in *A Hard Day's Night*. Criss-crossing the country in a shared coach, tour parties would often sleep in cheap hotels (or even rough on the coach), stop off in a makeshift and shared dressing room, and give their 'twice-nightly' performance on a spartan front-of-screen stage with a front-of-house staff ill-prepared for contemporary pop performance. As Martin Creasy notes in his record of the Beatles' UK touring days, these newly converted cinemas were barely fit for purpose:

> The sound systems were archaic, with most venues only set up for one microphone, and staff not trained to deal with the complexities of live shows. Spotlights would sometimes be shone on John instead of George, or Ringo instead of Paul, by the harassed and under-trained cinema staff.
>
> (2005: 57)

Even so, for want of alternative venues a third tour, 18 May–9 June, where Roy Orbison magnanimously ceded top billing, saw 14 of their 21-date performances once more take place around the country's picture houses (Lewisohn 1992: 109–12). By this point the screaming was completely drowning out the Beatles' set, and though the group were now important enough to be driven to gigs, the corollary saw their freedom of movement severely curtailed since they were confined to their dressing-room and slipped into and out of buildings.

With Epstein, a skilled promoter if not businessman, determined not to let the momentum slip, this (now potentially dangerous) state of affairs nonetheless endured into a fourth Autumn tour, beginning on 1 November. A sense of the atmosphere now being generated can be gleaned from Ray Coleman's coverage of the opening date:

> The problem at sedate Cheltenham is how to get the Beatles into the Odeon unscathed. Fans have been waiting outside the theatre since

10am, hoping for a glimpse of those famous hairstyles ... The Beatles' Austin [Princess] manages to weave through the thousands lining the streets and John, Paul, George and Ringo dart swiftly into their dressing rooms ... Getting them inside was like a military operation, requiring close links with police. Now on with the show ... What the Beatles are singing is unimportant. Fans rush up the gangways, arms outstretched, pleading "Paul! Paul!" The Beatles are unmoved and bash away.

(1963: 9)

Concluding at the Gaumont, Southampton on 13 December, cinemas comprised 23 of the tour's 34 venues (Lewisohn 1992: 127–33). Thus, in 1963, a hectic promotional year interspersed with trips (until 3 August) 'back to base' at Liverpool's Cavern Club, several radio and television spots, two albums and three stand-alone singles, the single largest investment for the Beatles to spread the word came via over 100 packed performances at 60 cinema bookings across the UK. It was only with their 1964 booking in the US and appearances at major venues housing five-figure audiences that their touring mode, and the nature of music touring itself, would, as Bill Harry notes, be 'completely revolutionised' (1992: 659). However, the incessant screaming such concerts generated made it clear that the fans had come not to hear but to *see* their idols, so it made (commercial) sense that the Beatles should now vacate the cinema stage to play instead up on its screen. In the process they also revolutionised the pop music film.

The life-span of Britain's pop music film sub-genre is roughly concurrent with what Arthur Marwick has termed 'the long Sixties' (1998: 7), a period also encompassing the life-span of the Beatles. According to Marwick, 'sometime between the early fifties and the early seventies a "cultural revolution" took place in Britain', leading to the creation of distinctive cultural artefacts, 'pop music (above all)' (1996: 13). Jeffrey Richards and Anthony Aldgate specify 1956–1958 as Britain's 'cultural watershed', witnessing 'the arrival of rock music from the United States' and 'the first steps towards the development of the distinctive youth culture that was to flow into the 1960s and took the form of protest against established canons of taste, decency and respectability' (1983: 111). Accompanying pop/rock music, cinema was central to this cultural transformation and transgression. Alongside Nicholas Ray's study of teenage alienation with James Dean's introspective *Rebel Without A Cause* (1955), the youthful rallying point would be sounded by Richard Brooks' pointed linking of juvenile delinquency with social deprivation in MGM's *Blackboard Jungle* (1955). Here the eleventh-hour deployment of Bill Haley's 'Rock Around the Clock' over the opening and closing credits helped both to spook the moral majority and, in the US, prompt huge film and soundtrack profits from an enthusiastic teenage fanbase. In the UK, though, the British Board of Film Censors (BBFC) afforded the film an X certificate – 'passed for exhibition to persons over the age of sixteen'[1] – thus (officially) barring it to its depicted audience.

However, for many underage teenagers this restriction, paralleling the film's depiction of adult impediment, merely acted as a socio-cultural challenge to rebel. Paul McCartney recalls helping 15-year-old George Harrison to 'bluff' his way into the film – only to be 'quite disappointed: all acting and talking!' (Beatles 2000: 21). Instead, for teenagers seeking cinema excitement, it was Columbia's hastily arranged spin-off musical *Rock Around the Clock* (Sears, 1956) that, trailing transatlantic tales of juvenile disorder, occasioned 'copycat' behaviour when shown around Britain, with teenage audiences dancing in the aisles and tearing out cinema seats. That, at least, was the press-enflamed depiction (Whitcombe 1972: 226–7): in reality, such visceral experiences depended on fortuitously being at a showing with the 'right' audience. Ringo Starr attended while holidaying with his grandparents on the Isle of Man: 'The film was sensational because the audience ripped up the cinema, which was great to watch. I didn't join in, because I was a sickly child; I was just so excited that they were doing it for me' (Beatles 2000: 36). By contrast, a more expectant John Lennon recalled his disappointment the night he attended in Bootle: 'Nobody was screaming and nobody was dancing. I'd read that everybody danced in the aisles. It must have all been done before I went. I was all set to tear up the seats too but nobody joined in' (Braun 1964: 35). Instead he had to sit through a tame and lifeless movie.

Even though the film's success led to Haley monopolising Britain's top thirty that September, incidents such as those witnessed by Ringo made rock'n'roll too hot to handle and so, again aping the American scenario, the wariness from major studios gave smaller independent companies the chance to move in and churn out bargain-basement fare for a hopefully quick killing. The use of current indigenous pop stars was understandable, a strategy to expand their star status (and thus maximise the financial returns) through a cross-media alliance of their films with associated record and sheet music releases, together with publicity generated through press, radio and television outlets. This move was indicative of the growing synergistic rapport within the British and increasingly global entertainment industries, but while the marketing and exhibition channels were carefully planned, little thought was given to aesthetic factors. Paul McCartney recalled the situation for the targeted teen audience: 'In those days it was a case of beggars can't be choosers. We were just desperate to get anything. Whatever film came out, we'd try to see it' (Beatles 2000: 28).

Here was a relatively untapped and potentially lucrative market. Nonetheless, adjudging teenage musical taste a volatile environment

– Haley's popularity quickly faded, his faux pas being to tour the UK and thus expose, in the (paunchy) flesh, a 'back-dated vaudeville act' (Cohn 1969: 21) – the producers of Britain's first pop music films diluted rock'n'roll with what they considered the more lasting and inclusive sounds of skiffle, jazz, even calypso. And so, just pipping E.J. Fancey Productions' *Rock You Sinners* (Kavanagh, 1957), a blatant exploitation piece crammed with bandwagon-climbing band leaders such as Tony Crombie and Art Baxter, came Anglo-Amalgamated's loosely-biographical *The Tommy Steele Story* aka *Rock Around the World* (Bryant, 1957). This was a film where Caribbean expositions charted the rise to fame of Britain's first pop-rocker, a mother-loving boy from Bermondsey and a non-threatening anti-dote to Elvis Presley. Commercially successful, it was swiftly pastiched in Butcher's *The Golden Disc* aka *The In-Between Age* (Sharp, 1958) 'star-ring' the charisma-challenged Steele epigone Terry Dene. It was then paro-died in Britannia Films' *Expresso Bongo* (Guest, 1959), an adaptation of Wolf Mankowitz and Julien More's sophisticated West End musical. The film version's titular teen sensation Bongo Herbert was played by Steele's successor and Britain's primary pop star of the pre-Beatles era, the peren-nial (now Sir) Cliff Richard.

Richard had already made his screen debut as a leather-jacketed 'J.D.' snarling an up-tempo version of 'Living Doll' in Alva Films' *Serious Charge* (Young, 1959), set like its forebears in the amoral kernel of Britain's burgeoning youth culture – and the launchpad for myriad early pop-rockers including the pre-Beatles Quarrymen – the jukebox-animated coffee bar.[2] Richard's opening films showcased the cinematic and commercial potential of the 'British Elvis', and just like Presley he was, largely through his subse-quent film depictions, swiftly 'tamed' for mainstream and thus more lucra-tive audience appeal. Richard epitomised national trends, for just as British cinema in the late-1950s introduced an edgy New Wave of Social Realism, so British pop music also changed, but in the opposite direction. Again, one can place a two-year watershed: Charlie Gillett pinpoints 1958, rock'n'roll having 'petered out' via the music industry's recuperation (1983: 256); Nik Cohn proposes 1960, 'a wipe-out' with early rockers dead, jailed, religious or, like post-Army Elvis, churning out 'awful ballads' (1969: 75).

This demise is both sonically and visually rendered in Cliff Richard's film trilogy of the early 1960s, *The Young Ones* (Furie, 1961), *Summer Holiday* (Yates, 1963) and *Wonderful Life* (Furie, 1964), all six-figure-budgeted widescreen and Technicolor productions from the major studio ABPC (Associated British Picture Corporation), all importing a musical grammar and choreography direct from heyday MGM American film musi-cals, all showing their teenagers as efficient and responsible citizens and all making a healthy profit with their broad family appeal (Glynn 2013:

48–68). With the US churning out similar safe and formulaic fare 'ranging' from *Gidget* (Wendkos, 1959) to *Beach Party* (Asher, 1963), and with trad jazz now the major vehicle for UK social protest, youth culture needed something different, something new, something of its own. Welcome to the screen, John, Paul, George and Ringo.

Notes

1 Introduced by the BBFC in 1951, the X certificate only had its age limit raised to eighteen in July 1970.
2 An early cinema influence: the Casbah Coffee Club in Liverpool where, on 29 August 1959, John, Paul, George (and Ken Brown) resurrected the Quarrymen, was so named because its owner, Pete Best's mother Mono, admired the film *Algiers* (Cromwell, 1938) and its star Charles Boyer's oft-imitated (but apocryphal) invitation to 'Come with me to ze Casbah' (Harry 1992: 135).

1 The Beatles and youth culture
A Hard Day's Night (1964)

This chapter explores a film that promises to place the viewer at the centre of a new youth culture phenomenon – Beatlemania. It emphasises how *A Hard Day's Night*, despite its genre-shifting expressions of youthful exaltation, achieved a rare cross-generational acceptance – the first of many 'dualities' at play. It shows the extent to which the Beatles are mediated – their first film, culminating in a television concert, employs a proliferation of photographs and camera screens but also utilises the methodologies and iconography of contemporary (pop) art practices. It examines how the Beatles are mythologised – long before the backlash prompted by John Lennon's comparison of the group with Jesus,[1] Lester intimates a quasi-religious status via art-house-inflected symbolism, implicitly situating the group as purveyors of a fresh and secular promise of fulfilment through their music's transgressive potential for sheer pleasure. This promise is shouted out with genuine conviction by Beatlemania's (predominantly) female fan-base who thus define alternative and independent values that mark them off from the adult world. Nonetheless, this new enraptured youth culture is skilfully marketed (including via this film), with the foregrounded Beatles b(r)and pushing all to become not just fans (or even worshippers) but also/especially consumers. Cinema and youth culture, from the off, are seen to combine to form a heavily monetised phenomenon.

Production and reception

On 29 October 1963, four days before the Beatles opened their fourth cinema-centred UK concert tour, Brian Epstein reached an agreement with United Artists for the group's feature film debut. Though the Beatles had barely registered in the US (only Del Shannon's cover of 'From Me to You' had charted, at number 77), Noel Rodgers, the British representative for United Artists Records, had witnessed the growing phenomenon soon labelled Beatlemania and was convinced that America would not long resist. When he ascertained that EMI had not covered film soundtracks in their contract with the Beatles, Rodgers approached George 'Bud' Ornstein, production head of United Artists' European film division, with the proposal that they offer Epstein a three-picture deal for the group, in essence solely to obtain three potentially profitable soundtrack albums. Thus, in its conception, the future acme of pop music cinema was – *pace* Technicolor Cliff Richard – identical to all its generic predecessors. With no artistic pretentions, here was a low-budget, low-tech exploitation movie existing only to milk the latest low-rated youth musical craze to the maximum.

Ornstein approached Walter Shenson, an independent American producer who, with fare such as the satirical Peter Sellers vehicle *The Mouse That Roared* (Arnold, 1959), had shown the ability to render British products accessible to the US market. Ornstein's brief to Shenson was simple: to deliver a film containing an album's worth of new songs. The Beatles, astute regarding their career development, had already turned down Epstein's proposal of a cameo debut in Tekli Productions' schoolgirl 'sexploitation' feature *The Yellow Teddy Bears* aka *Gutter Girls* (Hartford-Davis, 1963), less for the film's surrounding risqué content than for not wanting to sing others' songs or lose copyright on their own work (Glynn 2016: 139–42). They also did not want, in Lennon's words, to be 'stuck in one of those typical nobody-understands-our-music plots where the local dignitaries are trying to ban something as terrible as the Saturday Night Hop' (Carr 1996: 30). Given that this put-down perfectly summarises the Helen Shapiro-starring *It's Trad, Dad!*, it appears counter-intuitive that this very film's director, Dick (now Richard) Lester, was approached.

However, Lester, known to Shenson after being recommended by Sellers to direct the Grand Fenwick sequel *The Mouse on the Moon* (1963), instantly won the group's approval, less for his pop film work than for his association with Britain's madcap radio entertainment, *The Goon Show* (BBC Home Service, 1951–60). The Beatles, especially Lennon, loved the comedy short Lester had made with Goon members Sellers and Spike Milligan, the Academy Award-nominated *The Running, Jumping & Standing Still Film* (1959), and liked the idea of creating their own piece of slapstick surrealism. Also significant for his credibility, Lester, aged 32, was only half the average age (65 years 6 months) of those habitually entrusted with Hollywood youth pictures such as the Elvis Presley film cycle (Bean 1964: 12). With all parties happy, a standard low-budget ceiling of £200,000/$350,000 was agreed – with the Beatles' cut eventually negotiated up from Epstein's initial (ineptly negotiated) 7.5 to 20 percent of all net profits (Davies 2016: 573).

Lester brought along his regular cameraman Gilbert Taylor whilst the Beatles provided the film's musical director, their record producer George

Martin. Screenwriting duties were entrusted to Welsh-born but Liverpool-reared Alun Owen who, as well as having worked with Lester in television, had impressed the Beatles, especially McCartney, with his gritty depiction of Merseyside in the 'Armchair Theatre' drama *No Trams to Lime Street* (ITV, 1959). Owen spent time with the group to familiarise himself with their rapport and routine since it had been decided from the off that the film would constitute a caricatured 'day in the life', a fictionalised documentary of the Beatles' real-life reactions to their youth-fed celebrity. This faux-cinéma-vérité project lent itself to black-and-white photography, a format replicating the Beatles' footage now flooding press and television outlets, and one that, for Owen, fitted the quartet's personalities: 'They are immediate people and I knew from that that it couldn't be a colour film. The boys are essentially black and white people' (quoted in Harry 1992: 506).

Owen completed a generally approved first draft in late-January 1964. By February, though, a day in the life for the Beatles had changed – beyond all recognition. In Britain the group's success had been swift but incremental: in the US Beatlemania was instant and enveloping. In what constitutes the definitive fortnight in pop music history, the Beatles, with 'I Want to Hold Your Hand' bulleting from 73 to number 1 on the Billboard chart, had wowed the press from the moment they touched down at New York's airport on 7 February. Two days later 'these youngsters from Liverpool' had been watched on *The Ed Sullivan Show* by 73 million, not just the highest viewing figures ever for a television broadcast but 'possibly the most significant cultural event in post-war America' (Stanley 2013: 122). By the time they flew out on 21 February the Beatles had completely conquered US hearts (and purse-strings). With their mop-top image known from coast to coast and their full back-catalogue about to occupy all top-five positions on the Billboard singles chart, the Beatles had suddenly become the most bankable pop stars on the planet. And yet, in nine days' time, they were contractually obligated to start working on a rock-bottom-financed exploitation quickie.

Despite now having this unprecedented youth culture phenomenon to handle, all parties agreed to remain with existing arrangements, especially the documentary-style use of black and white (see Glynn 2005: 21–9). There was one agreed addition, though: following the enormous success of the Beatles' New York airport lounge press conference, Owen penned a press buffet scene allowing the boys to proffer similarly dazzling repartee. With speed of the essence, an experienced acting team was entrusted to deliver their sections with minimum fuss, allowing most attention to be focused on directing the pop star debutants – a situation helped by Owen's staccato script, which pragmatically limited the boys to one line of dialogue at a time. In the recording studio, the Beatles also delivered swiftly: in the week prior to filming they worked up the tapes of nine songs from which Lester would choose six to film.

On the morning of Monday 2 March, a train left Paddington Station platform 5, with John, Paul, George and Ringo plus the film crew all on board. From the outset they were besieged by hordes of frenzied fans: this disrupted production schedules but provided suitable raw material for the expedient Lester. In one early scene, for instance, he shot a crowd of screaming girls who had surrounded the Beatles' limo after a long day's shooting, footage knitted into the film which explains the continuity error where the boys wear different clothes on and off the train. Thus, at times the fictional documentary became factual – and/or vice versa. For the closing concert sequences, shot at London's Scala Playhouse again before genuinely rapturous fans, Lester employed six cameras shooting simultaneously as the Beatles performed, allowing John Jympson's subsequent editing to provide a visual energy commensurate with the music. The plot, perfunctory as it would be in all Beatles films, follows the group as they travel down to London to appear in a television variety show. Accompanying them are manager Norm (Norman Rossington) and road-manager Shake (John Junkin), plus Paul's grandfather (Wilfrid Brambell), a 'real mixer' who, after sowing disruption at a casino and press conference, needles Ringo into going AWOL, jeopardising the television appearance. After solo adventures culminating in his arrest, Ringo is freed just in time for the group to reach the studio and perform before an ecstatic audience. Show over, they are immediately rushed out to a helicopter and on to their next event.

The reception afforded *A Hard Day's Night* indicates a paradigm shift in the representation of 1960s youth culture. Firstly, cross-media success was record-breaking, with Noel Rodgers' coveted soundtrack songs excelling in all formats. The tie-in singles 'Can't Buy Me Love' and 'A Hard Day's Night' topped both the UK and US charts, while the accompanying album, the film's sole *raison d'être* and, in a pioneering move, entirely penned by Lennon-McCartney, achieved unparalleled results, topping the US album chart for 14 weeks, the UK chart for 21 weeks, and achieving global sales of close on four million, half from America (Coryton and Murrells 1990: 97). Pre-release demand was especially significant, as the momentum created by US radio previews led to advance orders of over two million album copies, ensuring the film's production budget had already been doubled in profits. This LP ferment fed back into film demand, with America alone demanding 700 prints, Britain 110, while globally a record 1500-plus prints were ordered. This led United Artists to announce boldly that, with under four weeks to edit and make copies, *A Hard Day's Night* would enjoy saturation exhibition with 'more prints in circulation than for any other pic in history' (Carr 1996: 47). Such was the demand for products associated with the

Beatles that *A Hard Day's Night* became the first motion picture in history to secure a profit while shooting was still in progress.

Uniquely for a pop music film, *A Hard Day's Night* was granted a Royal World Premiere on 6 July 1964 at the London Pavilion before HRH Princess Margaret – while an estimated 20,000 fans outside necessitated closing Piccadilly Circus (see Frontispiece). In America the film was officially premiered at the Beacon Theatre in New York on 12 August and the next day opened in 500 cinemas across the country – though entreaties for early showings had already brought in over half a million dollars. In addition to unparalleled publicity, the release was shrewdly timed just prior to the Beatles' 26-date (technically misnamed) 'First American Tour' from 19 August to 20 September, synergising with concert venues that, holding between 7000 and 23,000, dwarfed UK provincial picture houses. In total, the film's box-office profits would prove phenomenal, bringing in $5,800,000 in US rentals in six weeks, and a worldwide gross close on $14 million (Denisoff and Romanowski 1991: 138). Returning 40 times on its investment, here was youth culture monetised far beyond expectation. Not, though, beyond exportation. It merits clarification that, while *A Hard Day's Night* was/is categorised as a British film in that it employed British cast, crew and locations, its financing came from and therefore its profits went to United Artists, an American company and established a funding pattern for the rest of the decade.

Along with this unshakable commercial progress, the Beatles' debut film won near-unanimous plaudits. Richard Dyer has explained the power of 'stars' in terms of their ability not so much to represent particular social categories but rather to 'speak to dominant contradictions in social life – experienced as conflicting demands, contrary expectations, irreconcilable but equally held values – in such a way as to appear to reconcile them' (1992: 80). The critical reaction to *A Hard Day's Night* indicates that it effected just such an ideological reconciliation, notably captivating older, uncertain (predominantly male) writers. Britain's youth-oriented music press were – unsurprisingly – bedazzled. For Andy Gray in the *New Musical Express* (*NME*), 'Dick Lester has a great flair for comedy and the editing of the film is razor sharp, a major contribution to the success. But the Beatles have come through with flying colours. Whereas many pop stars sound unreal and even horrible when given films, the Beatles really punch them over with a naturalness that is refreshing and they look good throughout' (1964: 3). Equally charmed, though, were the country's august film journals. Despite the caveat that 'the pace is too frantic', the British Film Institute (BFI)'s *Monthly Film Bulletin* found *A Hard Day's Night* 'streets ahead in imagination compared to other films about pop songs and singers' ('*A Hard Day's Night* review' 1964: 121), while in its sister publication *Sight and Sound* – following a piece on François Truffaut's *La Peau Douce/Silken Skin* (1964) – Geoffrey

Nowell-Smith more broadly declared that, despite its 'casual camerawork' and 'non-acting', '*eppur si muove*: and yet it works', and works 'on a level at which most British films, particularly the bigger and more pretentious, don't manage to get going at all' (1964: 196–7).

Between Andy Gray's *NME* eulogy and the BFI's Galilean Latin, middlebrow magazines also heralded a youth culture game-changer. *The Spectator*'s Isobel Quigly, recalling the just-released *Wonderful Life*, concluded that the Beatles' 'whole style, not just of singing, but of behaving ... of taking things quizzically and giving as good as they get, makes Cliff Richard last week seem like a cream-fed domestic cat compared with a litter of perfectly groomed jaguars' (1964). In the national press, by contrast, the group's style of behaving drew not feline but lofty film comparisons. Cecil Wilson found the Beatles 'just as crazily inconsequential, just as endearingly insolent, just as infectiously pleased with themselves and – not consistently but here and there – just as funny as the Marx Brothers' (1964). Penelope Gilliatt, praising the group's 'pure comedy', saw 'four highly characterised people caught in a series of intensely public dilemmas but always remaining untouched by them, like Keaton, because they cart their private world around everywhere' (1964).

As much as the Buster Keaton comparison, the term 'highly characterised' is important here. British actor/director Jonathan Miller, referencing the youth-fearing *Village of the Damned* (Rilla, 1960), had already likened the identikit mop-tops to the 'Midwich Cuckoos' (Ingham 2006: 194), but here, for the so-far resistant older generation, the four-headed monster was transformed into distinct – and decent – individuals. Michael Thornton, who saw the film as possessing 'all the ingredients of good cinema – wonderful photography, imaginative direction, and excellent character performances', was typical in asserting the film's 'great surprise' as 'the extent to which the four boys emerge as personalities in their own right' (1964). Felix Barker (aged 46) proffered the perspective of 'many a parent' for whom 'a year's intensive propaganda from the nursery' had given 'a built in apathy'. Writing 'as a man who until this week didn't know Ringo from Paul or George from John (and cared rather less), let me join in the high pitched, frenzied screaming of teenage enthusiasm' (1964).

The US was similarly smitten. *Time* magazine, though not alone in finding 'the North Country slang impenetrable', considered 'this hairy musical romp' as 'one of the smoothest, freshest, funniest films ever made solely for the purposes of exploitation' with 'Beatlesong, frothy fiction, and an air of high-spirited improvisation almost as amusing as life itself' ('Yeah? Yeah, Yeah!' 1964). Equally, Bosley Crowther, previously hostile to pop music film formats, admitted his surprise that 'the new film with those incredible chaps, the Beatles, is a whale of a comedy' and a work 'much more sophisticated in theme and technique than its seemingly frivolous matter promises' (1964: 41). Andrew Sarris, in the ultimate critical soundbite, termed it 'the *Citizen Kane* of jukebox musicals', thought it 'a movie that works on every level for every kind of audience', anticipated Dyer in 'lik[ing] the Beatles at this moment in film history … because they express effectively a great many aspects of modernity that have converged inspiredly in their personalities', and joined others in discovering how 'each is a personable individual behind their collective façade of androgynous selflessness' (1964). *A Hard Day's Night* was also the recipient of two Academy Award nominations, Alun Owen for Best Original Screenplay and George Martin for Scoring of Music – Adaptation or Treatment. Pop fashions repeatedly change, but the film's reputation has, if anything, increased over time. In 1999 it was voted number 88 in the BFI's survey of the most significant 'culturally British' feature films (BBC News 1999). In 2005 *Time* magazine moved from its initial exploitation categorisation to rank it as one of the 'All-*Time* Top 100 Movies' (Corliss and Schickel 2005).

Celebrating youth culture

A Hard Day's Night celebrates the joy and exuberance of youth culture, a phenomenon embodied in the actions and attitudes of its adolescent adherents and young adult idols. The film's depth, though, resides in its willingness to investigate the status of this new-form celebrity and the media machinery that promotes it. Aware that it contributes to the mythologising of its stars, it simultaneously subjects the process to a (lightly handled) critical analysis. This doubleness permeates the film, a wrong-footing refusal to decide encapsulated in its paradoxical title and entrenched in its generic characteristics – both cutting-edge documentary realism and established musical comedy. Lyrically, songs like 'Can't Buy Me Love' explore ambivalent forms of emotional and/or economic exchange, a parallel to those operating between artist, audience and their unabashed exploitation film, while Lester's knowing use of verbal and photographic clichés repeatedly undermines the façade of cinematic realism. From the opening scenes the ostensible cinéma-vérité style is questioned, exposing the duality resultant from shooting in public spaces: are the running, falling and laughing Beatles acting or actually fleeing their ubiquitous fans, or are such distinctions redundant given their effect on the behaviour of the film's young extras?

Granted coveted behind-the-scenes access, Lester's 'process' movie explores responses to this unprecedented pop-cultural happening, both by the media machine (seemingly) for once caught off-guard, but also its effect on the boys themselves – and though largely luxuriating in the new phenomenon, Beatlemania is revealed in places to be a double-edged experience.

For George Melly 'they were victims not victors. They were as trapped as any working-class boy or girl in a dead-end job' (1972: 73). Whether or not the comparison convinces, the film's opening signals a generic distinction from standard rags-to-riches pop star biopics like *The Tommy Steele Story*. Here running towards the audience are identifiable young celebrities (hence all credits are left to the film's end), already experiencing the vicissitudes of stardom. Though their omnipresent incarceration is downplayed, one can still infer Lester's representation of 'revolutionaries in a goldfish bowl' (Gelmis 1971: 316).

The film's claims to present a 'realistic' insight to life on the road for the Beatles are both supported and undermined by a comparison to the concurrent work commissioned by Granada Television and shot by American independent filmmakers Albert and David Maysles, an 'instant documentary' which captured the impact made by the Beatles on that February breakthrough tour of the US (McElhaney 2009: 65–7). Now existing in at least five versions, *Yeah! Yeah! Yeah! New York Meets the Beatles* (ITV, tx. 12 February 1964) aka *The Beatles in America* (CBS, tx. 13 November 1964) aka *What's Happening: The Beatles in the USA*, presents a number of scenes very similar to *A Hard Day's Night*: the airport press conference, the hotel and car sieges, even a train journey and escape to a nightclub (the latter a scene copied by Owen?). There are, however, significant differences. The Maysles documentary shows not only the Beatles' performances to besotted fans but the relentless peddling of their wares to radio stations – not only the smoking and drinking but also the girls being smuggled at night into their rooms. *A Hard Day's Night* is, by contrast, clearly a fictionalised – and sanitised – version of events, its propagandistic function rendering spurious any concerted comparison with raw documentary practice.

Similarities with fictional film formats promise more. Bob Neaverson sees *A Hard Day's Night* as a 'cinematic bastard' but, rather than evoking the interwar amalgam of cine-variety, stresses that 'Lester and Owen's narrative construction and pacing is, in effect (if not intention), closer to that of the French "new wave" than to any previous British or American pop musical' (1997: 17). Why, though, the 'not intention' caveat? Lester openly admired Jean-Luc Godard, Alain Resnais and François Truffaut (di Franco 1978: 37), and technical parallels, as with the use of a hand-held camera, freeze frames and jump cuts, abound in *A Hard Day's Night*. Such effects at times link back to the frantic practices of silent film comedy (cf. the Keystone Cops chase from the police station), but the modulations of the *Cahiers du Cinéma* collective marry equally with the Beatles' new star charisma – Ken Hanke sees Lennon as offering a 'British version of Jean-Paul Belmondo' (1989: 270); and with their starker musical compositions – Bob Stanley notes how 'the limpid minor-key melancholy of 'And I

Love Her' recalls George Delarue's score for *Jules et Jim* [Truffaut, 1962]' (2013: 125).

Above all, though, *A Hard Day's Night*'s cinematic correlation of the Beatles' songs advances pop music on film to new levels of sophistication. The opening title track immediately signals how the film will repeatedly avoid imitative diegetic performance, while a break with conventional presentation models is underlined in the early train-carriage rendition of 'I Should Have Known Better'. As musical instruments suddenly, surreally replace the Beatles' deck of cards, the song's articulation both adheres to and avoids the diegetic mode, removing any generic consistency and reinforcing an alternative, 'duplicitous' viewing strategy. Primarily, however, the filming that accompanies 'Can't Buy Me Love', creating 'a definitive short ballet of youthful high spirits' (Sinyard 2010: 38), constitutes the unmistakable advance, the formal paradigm shift for pop music on film. Coming after half-an-hour of intensifying claustrophobia, structurally the song signifies an enormous release of energy. When Ringo sees a door marked 'Fire Escape' the sign works like a signal, sending the group hurriedly down the external staircase onto the field below.

The sequence that follows takes its inspiration directly from Lester's *The Running, Jumping & Standing Still Film*. As the Beatles caper in Goonlike abandon, suddenly freed from the treadmill of nationwide touring, Lester and Gilbert Taylor employ diverse film speeds and camera angles to convey the quartet's musical liberation. When the boys jump over discarded props, the film momentarily accelerates to aid their rush into the open air. An aerial shot follows one of them up and down a long path but eschews a terminal 'sight gag' – the sense of achieved release is sufficient reward. When filming joins the group dancing together, Paul breaks the actors' taboo by rushing up to the camera and smiling out at the audience – a moment of unbounded and spontaneous elation. Not all these movements are captured on the hoof, however: the slow-motion shots of John, Paul and George jumping downwards pointedly reference the group's extant iconography, in particular Fiona Adams' celebrated photo of the leaping quartet behind Euston Station (employed on the cover of their first British EP, July 1963's 'Twist and Shout'). Altogether, though, it works – magnificently. For Andrew Sarris this sequence of 'the Beatles on a spree is one of the most exhilarating expressions of high-spirits I have seen on the screen' (1964). It is, indeed, the ultimate cinematic catharsis.

Despite such innovation, the Beatles' first movie must also be read as a traditional musical comedy. The group top the bill of a variety show including Lionel Blair and his dancers, operetta singers, even Derek Nimmo and his performing doves. This may seem backdated but was in fact a realistic entourage – as Michael Braun reported on their recent tour of France: 'Shortly after midnight the Beatles were introduced, but then a juggling act came on stage' (1964: 74). Again, though, it works, as the formulae of a backstage musical grant (fictional) access to both the public and private lives of the stars. Why shift from a tried and trusted strategy, well suited to the production company's aims of demonstrating the Beatles' confident musicianship and differentiating their individual personalities? Nonetheless, within this established sub-genre, *A Hard Day's Night* still demonstrates its youth culture credentials and registers its inherent modernity by removing the backstage show from a theatrical, or even cinematic context (as offered by Cliff Richard in *Wonderful Life*). Here we are thrust into the electronic – and at the time innovative, relatively unknown – processes of live television transmission. It is a further duality: a traditional backstage musical set amidst 'the white heat of technology'. We see the Beatles constantly mediated through a camera viewfinder or control-room monitors as the new power of television is everywhere foregrounded and fetishised (see Figure 1.1).

It is an entirely apposite presentation since the small screen had become the familiar (black-and-white) medium of the Beatles. The UK fanbase, when not squeezed into provincial cinemas, had enjoyed rare access to their idols via the group's televised appearances on just such variety shows. Fifteen million watched them top the bill on *Sunday Night at the London Palladium* (ITV, tx. 13 October 1963), 26 million saw their royalty-baiting appearance on the *Royal Variety Performance* (ITV, tx. 11 November 1963), while their record-breaking appearances on *The Ed Sullivan Show* (CBS, tx.

Figure 1.1. A Hard Day's Night – the mediation of youth culture.

9 and 16 February 1964) had provided their passport to acceptance across the US (Glynn 2005: 65). With cameras often present in shot, the film's mise-en-scène draws attention to the process of recording, making us aware how everything concerning the foursome is electronically orchestrated. They are revealed as young but consummate performers whose act is universalised by the newly dominant and democratising medium. The Beatles were the first group to be extensively 'sold' through television and *A Hard Day's Night* does not stray from that proven strategy.

The film does, however, incorporate other visual media in its attempt to 'capture' the excitement and significance of the Beatles. From its opening scene where the boys hide in a photo-booth, through the recreations of their Fiona Adams images, and on to its conclusion when grandfather McCartney's bogus stills rain down from the helicopter, the Beatles are repeatedly reproduced in photographic form. It is a deluge of images to parallel the film's staccato, cut-up, literally 'clichéd' style. A deluge but also a dilution: the film reiterates how the reality of the Beatles escapes the medium, our consumption being only of a simulacrum, a symbol mass-produced at myriad removes with, as Catterall and Wells note, those final images 'scattering *faked* autographed photos from the skies and, by extension, into cinemagoers' laps everywhere' (2001: 14). This is a commercially-driven proliferation. Written on the helicopter door from which those photographs cascade is not only the Beatles' name but also the logo for British European Airways (BEA), and the way its corporate acronym nestles within 'BEAtles' signals the unabashed marketing imperative (and product placement) of the whole Beatles project. Nonetheless, one can also detect a more implicit mythologising. The rotorcraft itself, taking the Beatles up into the heavens, offers a closing image redolent of the opening to another film illustrating the impact of youth cultures, music and fashion on a rapidly changing landscape, Federico Fellini's *La Dolce Vita* (1960). There, a helicopter lifts a giant statue of Christ the Redeemer across the Roman skyline. Here Lester more subtly, intertextually intimates what Lennon would later stupidly, internationally tell; that the Beatles were replacing Jesus as the dominant icon of the airways/airwaves.

Elsewhere fine art imagery comes into play. As the Lionel Blair dancers practise to 'I'm Happy Just to Dance with You', visible behind them are a series of blown-up photographic images of beetle-like insects – exactly the play on word and image that surrealist artist Max Ernst would effect in his 1968 Beatles sketches (Evans 1984: 131). Photography coheres with brash pop art practices when, during the press conference, the switch from a posing George to the proof sheet shots appearing across and down the screen offers a repetition mirroring the industrial process that globally disseminated the group's image – as on the film's UK publicity posters and soundtrack album cover (see Figure 1.2). Here, in Andy Warhol-style, is a celebration of the visual rhythm of contemporary 'packaging', with the boys as manufactured as cans of Campbell's Soup. Simultaneously, though, with their subtle individuating differences, the shots celebrate variation within standardisation. Here is a further doubleness as the accumulating detail allows an increased sense of character recognition while the image rhythm veers towards abstraction. Again, the message is conveyed through the medium: the mechanical image may be repeatedly consumed, but the real Beatles evade us. As Jon Lewis notes, 'their inaccessibility is held up as the logical extension of stardom: the scrapbook of images is as close to them as we will ever get. Stylistically, Lester demystifies stardom; thematically he glorifies it' (1992: 89).

The cessation of narrative flow to focus on George demonstrates how image/appearance/look was essential to this 'selling' of the Beatles. The early prime strategy of manager Brian Epstein had been a repackaging of the group to broaden their public acceptability, a move largely achieved through the Beatles' carefully managed fashion sense. Before signing with Epstein the group wore rock'n'roll leather jackets and blue jeans – the look of Elvis Presley in *King Creole* (Curtiz, 1958) and even Cliff Richard in *Serious Charge*. Aware of the associations of such dress with juvenile delinquency, Epstein had persuaded the boys (without undue resistance) to don their new Pierre Cardin-inspired 'Beatle suits' and Cuban-heeled 'Beatle boots'. It was a smart(-casual) move since, as Nigel Whiteley points out, their single-breasted jackets had a dual denotation: 'the aim of the Beatle

Figure 1.2. A Hard Day's Night – hey there, Georgie boy.

suit was to strike a balance between rebellion and respectability – rebellious-
ness to appeal to youth, respectability to soothe the parents – an aim that
was successful' (1987: 102). Aided by *A Hard Day's Night*, this new dress-
code not only rescued the group from a narrow image of youth-oriented
aggression into one of cross-generational acceptability, but it also replaced
a predominantly American iconography with a more Anglo-European sense
of theatrical costume.

This fashion realignment is highlighted in the film's showbiz setting,
which allows the Beatles several costume changes and make-up close-ups.
These situations emphasise their distinctive suits and hairstyles, but also
their comfortable position in mainstream variety performances. Their form-
fitting uniforms, created by Dougie Millings, accompany every song in the
film with their crease-free crisp lines as flawless as the music, the sole con-
cession to rehearsal mode visible in John's loosened shirt top button during 'If I Fell'.[2] This new 'Beatles look' is shown to be at the forefront of
public consciousness, and (replicating the February US tour) their haircuts
form the most common subject for bemused (older) journalists' questions at
the press conference. Deflationary criticisms are deflected with humour, as
when a mature tweed jacket's question, 'What would you call that hairstyle
you're wearing?' gets the answer from George, 'Arthur'. This Arthur hair
is the visual aspect most emphasised in the film's attendant material culture
and its closing credits when identically framed close-up photos of all four
band members are overlaid so quickly that it becomes almost impossible
to distinguish anything but the hairstyle – the (in)famous front-combed
'Beatle mop-top'.

Elsewhere, though, the film visually nuances the Beatles' individuality in their otherwise unifying dress sense, with John donning his Greek
fisherman's hat, George wearing stylish turtlenecks and Ringo bedecked
with jewellery. Add in Paul regularly getting out his comb, and the group
reveal a natural narcissism that, as Steven Stark notes, in its time helped
'change the way men feel, the way men look, and the way men think about
the way they look' (2005: 3). It must be stressed, though, that this new
youth culture styling was not uniformly accepted. Decidedly less hyper-
masculine than the late-1950s leather-jeans-and-quiff look of the Marlon
Brando-James Dean cohort, or even America's concurrent Chino-trousered
crew-cut 'preppy' look, many young males (especially in the US) decried
the Beatles for a 'prissy' – again sanitised – appearance, carefully engi-
neered to be less threatening for young female fans (Hewitt 2011: 59). This
also prompted wider generational concerns that the group's success signalled 'a troubling contemporary turn to a more androgynous look' (Gregg
2017: 26). These concerns would only have been reinforced by the claim
of German photographer Astrid Kirchherr that her original 'Beatle-cut' for

boyfriend Stuart Sutcliffe – a key moment in Beatles iconography recreated in both the poorly impersonated *The Birth of the Beatles* (Marquand, 1979) and cogently performed *Backbeat* (Softley, 1994) – was modelled on French actor Jean Marais' Oedipus in *Le Testament d'Orphée/The Testament of Orpheus* (Cocteau, 1960), thus rooting the newly dominant styling in European queer culture. With long hair especially associated with effeminacy, from top to toe the Beatles challenged traditional notions of masculinity, presenting for the young a bold and progressive image that 'explored the fluidity of gender' (Stark 2005: 3).

Such (anachronistically termed) pronouncements may seem counterintuitive in a film seemingly so centred on – and sold on – the Beatles' heteronormative sex appeal. A scene of Lennon in a hotel bathtub playing with his submarine may presage future war satires, but his topless appearance primarily presents a moment to relish for the young (largely female) fan gaze. More concertedly *A Hard Day's Night* adopted the ploy of all pre-Cliff Richard British pop music films by eschewing any romantic ties for the male stars. Thus, ignoring Lennon's August 1962 marriage to Cynthia Powell, as did all branches of the publicity machine, the film's narrative bolstered the fantasy then feeding Beatlemania that these four fab guys were still at the (safely distanced) disposal of their adoring female fans. So did its music, as in the Everly Brothers-inflected ballad 'If I Fell' which calculatedly projected a fragile availability. This is not to downplay the Beatles' rampant heterosexuality, which is emphasised by their constant interest in girls, be it schoolgirls on trains, studio make-up artists and dancers, office secretaries or girls in the street, and is enhanced by the comparative physical unattractiveness of those around them: no other young adult males appear; Norm and Shake take no obvious interest in the opposite sex; the middle-aged men encountered at the television studios, notably the show's director (Victor Spinetti) and his floor manager (Robin Ray) are all played as camp and, arguably worse still, have cut-glass middle-class accents. These over-blown gay characters, 'objects of ridicule' who 'exist only for comic relief and, no doubt, to reaffirm the Fab Four's heterosexuality', lead Stephen Bourne to denounce *tout court* 'the film's homophobia' (1996: 184–5).

Such criticism, however, is arguably harsh as more implicit and increasingly accommodating gay references can be found throughout *A Hard Day's Night*, predominantly centred on John. During the group's train journey, John flutters his eyelashes at the irate commuter – named Johnson in Owen's screenplay – and asks for a kiss; his theatre exchange with an actor in Regency dress opens with 'gear costume' and, after the gay-inflected offer to 'swap', ends with a suggestive 'Cheeky!'; in make-up, though sporting a fake beard, he introduces himself as 'Betty'; the accusation from grandfather McCartney that 'you're all a bunch of sissies', is answered by

John with 'you're just jealous'; when Paul accuses the television director of marital infidelity with his young blonde assistant, John, seemingly more tuned in to his sexual persuasion, says 'I bet he hasn't even got a wife, look at his sweater!' As Ann Shillinglaw notes, Lennon's 'comfortable knowledge of gay codes as a sign of coolness become a part of the Beatle's [*sic*] cultural contribution' (1999: 129).

A similar low-key knowingness is displayed in images of the Beatles' fanbase as young men clearly join the girls in chasing after their idols and screaming at their concerts. George Harrison recalled how, during the January 1964 shows in Paris – where Alun Owen joined them for final observations of their routine – 'a bunch of slightly gay-looking boys were hanging around the stage door shouting "Ringo! Ringo!"' (Beatles 2000: 112). One can surmise that some of the young male fans interspersed in the film's crowds (*pace* future Genesis drummer/singer Phil Collins) are also gay. None, though, are overblown objects of ridicule or comic relief. *A Hard Day's Night* effects a total and untrammelled market penetration.

Potential gay readings combine with fashion in a key scene that proclaims a new, indeed iconoclastic, youthful independence. While *A Hard Day's Night* is itself a commodification of the Fab Four, the film does not baulk at interrogating such cynically programmed processes and makes an astute critique of the merchandising of youth when Beatles insouciance counters the hyper-tense Simon (Kenneth Haigh), an advertising executive looking to identify and exploit the teenage market – and another character targeted by Bourne as 'camp' (1996: 184). When George wanders into an office and is mistaken for the company's latest male model, his protestations are dismissed by Simon as an affectation: 'You don't have to do all the old adenoidal glottal stuff and carry on for our benefit!' Simon is disconcerted when he realises that George is 'a natural', informing his secretary that 'you know by now that phoneys are much easier to handle'. George's job would be to give his opinion on some clothes for teenagers: 'not your real opinion, naturally. It'll be written out and you'll learn it.' In what seems like a jibe from the classical actor to the novice – an in-joke on Owen's staccato script – Simon/Haigh asks George/George if he can 'read': 'I mean lines, ducky. Can you handle lines?' Narratively, the style-guru reveals a patronising parasitism. While earning a good living from teenage fashion, Simon does nothing to conceal his contempt for the younger generation and their culture. 'Give him whatever it is they drink: Cocarama?' he tells his assistant, Adrian (another overblown gay depiction from Julian Holloway).

When George is given the shirts to look at and Simon informs him that 'you'll like these. You'll really "dig" them. They're "fab" and all those other pimply hyperbole', the film foregrounds the processes whereby rebellious language is rendered safely mainstream. Unsure of the youth culture discourse he is aiming to influence, Simon is bewildered when George dismisses their new range of shirts as 'dead grotty,' but asks that the word be noted for Susan, the agency's 'real trend-setter'. This exchange encapsulates a perfect paradigm of the life-cycle for new and 'trendy' language – a word or phrase, originating with youth people, is incorporated into celebrity discourse, before perishing on the calculating lips of advertising. Simon is horrified when Harrison rejects their resident teenage icon Susan as 'a drag, a well-known drag'. In a move exposing the perceived transience of the new fashions, Simon checks his calendar: no, there remain at least three weeks before trends change and so George and his 'utterly valueless opinions' are sent packing. 'The new thing,' he retorts, 'is to care passionately and to be right wing'. Harold Wilson's narrow October 1964 General Election victory with the UK's Labour Party would prove the professional's error of judgement in the political sphere, while George's casual exit ('I don't care!') shows him wrong on the current personal stance. Primarily, though, the whole scene serves to show that George, like the other Beatles, is 'real', 'a natural', and not just a product of marketing – which is, as *A Hard Day's Night* repeatedly demonstrates, both true and not true.

The scene is adroitly cast since Haigh (who declined a cast listing) had portrayed working-class anti-hero Jimmy Porter in the 1956 West End premiere of John Osborne's *Look Back in Anger*, and his stand-off here with Harrison emphasises how, in contrast to the frequent negativity if not hatefulness emanating from Osborne and Co., the Beatles offered a more cheerful sense of rebellion, an alternative and affable arrogance. As Lester noted on *Hollywood U.K.* (BBC1, 1993): 'I think they were the first to give a confidence to the youth of the country which led to the disappearance of the Angry Young Men with a defensive mein.' George's altercation is just one of several set-piece scenes where the Beatles confront older authority figures – and confidently play their way to victory. The last comes in their dealings with Spinetti's highly-strung and short-tempered television director, whose final complaint that 'once you're over thirty, you're past it. It's a young man's game!' acknowledges that the Beatles' appearance is a coup for his career, not theirs. They now possess the cultural capital and so can perform on their own terms.

The first and most blatant generational stand-off occurs during the train journey down to London when the Beatles encounter Johnson, the 'twice-a-week' first-class ticket holder who asserts his authority by closing the window and turning off Ringo's radio. With his bowler hat, club tie and regimental moustache, here is an unmistakable figure of the Establishment, the older, parental hegemony. He, though, not the Fab Four, is shown up as the impolite and intransigent adversary. It is he who swears, referring to their radio as 'that damn thing!' The Beatles try to articulate the rights of young people in a democratic society – four out of five want the window open – but to no avail. He answers with 'I fought the war for your sort', to which Ringo replies 'Bet you're sorry you won' – a (much-quoted) exchange that encapsulates changing societal dynamics.

Implicit in Johnson's rebuke is a generational anger at the recent demise of National Service, i.e. military conscription, a compulsory (and largely dreaded) part of young British men's post-war experience until abolished at the end of 1960 – the last recruits only leaving the armed forces in May 1963. Its removal undoubtedly saved the fledgling Beatles, since Ringo and John (and Pete Best and Stuart Sutcliffe) would otherwise have been eligible for Service in 1961 (Lang 2009: 11–12). With forces-trained Johnson impervious to reasoning, the Beatles do not fight back but resort to humour, softening the role to which he has consigned them by acting not as juvenile delinquents but mischievous schoolboys who want their ball back. The scene also offers a cinematic correlation to the societal shift being enacted. Until now *A Hard Day's Night* has adhered to the tenets of realism, but suddenly the group appear outside the carriage window gurning and cycling as the train is in motion. Here, we realise, is an exploration of the fluidity of genre: the film, like its heroes, will not comply with expectations.

Set on a train, redolent of both containment and movement, this early exchange signals a burgeoning phenomenon: the ending of the age of deference. As with their new fashion, this was not well received by all. Ann Scott-Jones, for instance, working for the *Daily Mail*, questioned the film's 'total remorselessness': 'This is a comedy without one twinge of pity for human beings, particularly the old. *A Hard Day's Night* is brilliant, fast, funny and distinctly frightening. I had thought of the Beatles as witty, talented, charming boys, but they are also as hard as old iron' (1964). The critic could have broadened her frame of reference, since the commuter, like the later executive and director, represents the waning influence not just of age but also class. Johnson clearly feels that the Beatles, despite their sartorial neatness, are socially inferior and instructs them to take their radio 'into the corridor or some other part of the train where you so obviously belong!' This was another aspect of Britain that mattered for Lester, an 'outsider looking in':

> The general aim of the film was to present what was apparently becoming a social phenomenon in this country … You must accept that this is a film based on a class society. It is difficult for someone coming from America, where there is a society based on money, to realise the strength … I mean a society that was still based on privilege – privilege by schooling, privilege by birth, privilege by accent, privilege by

speech. They were the first people to attack this … they said if you want
to do something, do it. You can do it.

(quoted in di Franco 1978: 5)

Here Lester created the original screen model for youthful independence,
strength and self-confidence – the cinematic celebration of 'boy power'.

This empowerment is also at play in the film's press conference sequence –
itself a staple of the British pop music film, framing the young star in *The
Tommy Steele Story*, undercutting the older star (Yolande Donlan) in *Expresso
Bongo*. Amplifying the face-offs with Simon and Spinetti, here the sequence
investigates how a commercially oriented 'artistic' generation – the middle-
class media professional – tries to exploit and recuperate this latest youth culture craze. Demonstrating a media machine literally feeding off the Beatles'
fame, the boys struggle to get hold of any food and drink at the reception sup-
posedly held in their honour, while the press gorge themselves so busily they do
not even notice the group leaving. The sequence foregrounds the quick-witted
responses of the Beatles, a display of satirical skill that immediately elicited
those critical comparisons with the 1930s Marx Brothers. Socially, though, it
plays out a confrontation between the values of the 1950s and 1960s.

Where, for instance, a Tommy Steele would sit quietly and reply politely
to the condescending questions of the bourgeois press, the Beatles spar,
they answer back. The journalists' different social class is evident from
their accents, their patronising manner, and (again especially) their fashion
sense – two women in flowery hats seem straight from a debutantes' catalogue – which motivates their consequent obsession with the Beatles' own
appearance. Faced with the Fab Four (and many were real journalists roped
in for the sequence) they constitute a class and a mind-frame suddenly
exposed as off the pace. As the Beatles run verbal rings around the writers,
they proclaim a generational victory – and yet (*pace* Scott-Jones) they do
so sociably, with a smile. By contrast, Paul's fictional grandfather, with his
unstinting scamming, Irish nationalism, accusations of police brutality –
and Brambell's rag-and-bone man 'baggage' from *Steptoe and Son* (BBC,
1962–74) – constitutes the film's (senior) delinquent: *his* is the stance as
hard as any old iron. The Beatles may mock the predictability of the para-
sitic press but, in spite of the strains placed on them by their celebrity status,
they remain generally friendly towards others, unaltered by their constant
presence in the spotlight. They are the good guys, the effulgent four.

Exploring Beatlemania

The Beatles' stand-offs are, significantly, centred on male authority figures.
Only two female characters have more than a single line to speak in the film.

At the television studio Millie (Anna Quayle), perhaps a figure of back-stage importance, speaks vacuously in a vaguely Pinteresque scene of mis-recognition with John. The second speaks sensibly but, as Simon's office secretary (Alison Seebohm), holds negligible evident power or influence. Thus, in *A Hard Day's Night* the individual female is ostensibly rendered inarticulate or inaudible, or else remains silent. This passive stance is con-sistent with the title track's patriarchal paradigm, where the male singer's responsible labour – 'I've been working like a dog' – is rewarded by the attentions of his waiting woman – 'When I'm home / Feeling you hold-ing me tight'. All changes, though, if gender depictions are considered at a collective level. In audio-visual terms there is a greater female presence on screen than male, and the Beatles' fanbase, seemingly a high-pitched pervasion whose behaviour was regularly described/dismissed in the press as mass 'hysteria' – a distinctly gendered term 'loaded with negative conno-tations' (de Kloet and van Zoonen 2007: 322) – is nonetheless here shown as signifying more pro-actively. The fans' affective power is omnipresent: they chase the Beatles at the film's opening and persistently scream out their desires at the conclusive concert that revels in its revelation of a youth culture female-led and unleashed, and that offers a gender-balancing mani-festation of 'girl power'.[3] This ending merits detailed analysis.

With the camera focusing on the balcony's young audience before the music starts, the final televised show constitutes cinema's first concerted examination of the relationship between fans and their pop music idols – and again it plays two ways. The rapport needs, of course, to be contextu-alised within the decade-old development of a distinct teenage culture in western society. Rock'n'roll was central to its articulation, and especially its exploitation, with the knowledge now garnered of an attention economy enlisting a form of 'hysteria' in order to sell fan merchandise – the 'pub-lic wants what the public gets' model. Thus, the 'overnight success' of the Beatles in the US was in truth carefully orchestrated, with the fans' passion (and spending) stoked by press and radio reports of the Beatlemania that had just swept the UK. This fan manipulation is redeployed in microcosm at the climax to *A Hard Day's Night*.

The concert begins with an excitement-building delayed entry. There are shots of girls screaming, and a view from the back of the stalls revealing how distant and indistinct the stage appears. The opening chords of 'Tell Me Why' are rhythmically matched by a close-up of four large background posters, each a multiple exposure of a Beatle jumping. The pose replays the jumps seen during the group's 'Can't Buy Me Love' frolics, intimating that even their moment of apparent escape has been caught and commodified. Another view down onto the balcony leads into four separate close-ups of individual female fans, each clearly mouthing, in order, 'Paul', 'Ringo',

'John' and (fact melding with fiction, the future Pattie Boyd Harrison shouting) 'George'. It is only after this democratic presentation of frieze and frenzy, a full 15 seconds into the chorus, that the film presents for the non-diegetic audience a mid-shot of the boys on stage.

The montage of wall-mounted images links effectively with the group's distinct performance style with its static poses (unlike 'Snake Hips' Elvis or the shimmying Shadows), then transitions into a shot from the control room, a reminder of the Beatles' constant mediation. Alternating close-ups of a girl close to fainting with Paul, George and John are followed by a slow tracking shot behind Ringo's drums, a camera movement which presents, for the first time on screen together, the fans and group in performance mode. Offering a chaste erotics of art, it constitutes the single crowning moment in *A Hard Day's Night* and, I would contend, the apotheosis of 1960s pop culture. Lacking the traditional romantic sub-plot, the final 'boy-girl' union is revealed as this meeting of exultant fans and excited players (the on-stage Beatles appearing here at their happiest and most fulfilled). Within the agreed perimeters of the stage and auditorium, the concert freshly delivers on the musical's longstanding generic and ideological function as, in Richard Dyer's formulation, 'a gospel of happiness' (1992: 61).

It is a gospel with transatlantic applications. For John Mundy, *A Hard Day's Night* adopts 'an almost ethnographic approach to a phenomenon which was central in the reconstruction of British identity in the mid-1960s', i.e. the emergent 'Swinging London', and achieves this through Lester's 'hand-held' aesthetic which 'implicates its young audience within a world which seems occupied as much by themselves as by the Beatles' (1999: 172). It is a symbiotic relationship at moments personalised by Lester's filming. During its sweeps across the concert audience, the camera comes to rest four times on a round-faced blond-haired fan, her cheeks streaked with tears. Lester has referred to her as 'the White Rabbit' (quoted in di Franco 1978: 31), an affectionate sobriquet for a young woman whose own nervous pleasure is given up to the four men she may well continue to follow far into adulthood (see Figure 1.3). Much as the filming of the Beatles performing emphasises the tight, communal nature of their music, so this young woman seems to have lost all sense of personal identity. Though singled out, she is part of a wave of adulation, safely distant from the figures on stage and yet their necessary completion. As Hannah Ewens notes of female pop fans from Beatlemaniacs through to Beliebers: 'To be a fan is to scream alone together. To go on a collective journey of self-definition' (2019: 5–6). What a 'fangirl' such as 'the White Rabbit' is not, though, any more than the Beatles themselves, is a victim. Such communal self-defining makes her instead a youthful agent for social subversion.

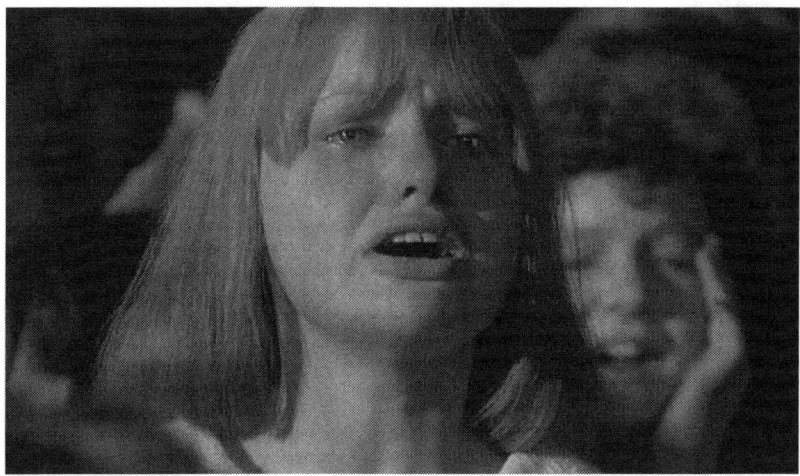

Figure 1.3. A Hard Day's Night – Alice in Wonderland.

In their pioneering discussion of Beatlemania as manifested in white, middle-class America, Barbara Ehrenreich, Elizabeth Hess and Gloria Jacobs saw such female fans as expressing a form of playful sexuality, shocking in the context of the then-dominant American codes, and which allowed an opening for the development of alternative roles for women during the later 1960s: 'To abandon control – to scream, faint, dash about in mobs – was, in form if not in conscious intent, to protest the sexual repressiveness, the rigid double standard of female teen culture. It was the first and most dramatic uprising of *women*'s sexual revolution' (1992: 85). Again, why the 'not in conscious intent' caveat? The so-called 'hysteria' recorded in Lester's film – and replicated across the US – possessed an intensity far in excess of earlier Frank Sinatra and Elvis Presley fan movements, and 'the White Rabbit', like her fellow transatlantic Baby Boomers, is here exploiting the Beatles as much as she is being exploited. This is far from the patronising, even vilifying, presentation of a critic such as Paul Johnson, for whom (infamously) the Beatles' fans were 'enslaved', 'grovelling' agents of 'anti-culture' and 'the least fortunate of their generation, the dull, the idle, the failures' (1964). The behaviour captured by Lester can be read not only as a cathartic release of sexual energy, but rather the para-linguistic articulation of a refusal to be socialised into a subjective 'adoring' gender role. This is the positive assertion of a teenage collective power, able to dictate through her/their purchasing power the fate of her/their proffered idols – the 'public gets what the public wants' model. Perhaps more importantly, it signifies the ability of the female fans to occupy public spaces and adopt transgressive behaviour beyond the bounds of genteel conformity.[4]

'The White Rabbit' is fully active in her relationship to the text, and *A Hard Day's Night* registers and shares her productivity throughout the final concert. After edited versions of 'If I Fell' and 'I Should Have Known Better' – the latter's closing sweeps nuancing the gender revolution argument since it highlights several young boys amidst the general mayhem – the set climaxes with the Beatles' signature tune, the affirmative and altruistic ode to joy 'She Loves You'. Both textually and contextually, it is the only viable concluding number. The song, released back in August 1963, would remain, with 1.5 million sales, the group's most successful UK single: it topped the US charts in March 1964, and by the time of filming was already being viewed as a landmark recording. Notably, it had concluded the group's October 1963 *London Palladium* set, the reaction to which, making front-page news in Britain's national press, brought full (if belated) recognition of Beatlemania.

Lester wisely stays with that running order. The performance of 'She Loves You' also answers the question prompted by *A Hard Day's Night*'s opening: just why are these young fans behaving in this manner? A film that begins with the effects of Beatlemania ends with its single definable cause. One could push the structural closure further. Much as the first shots visually present a mass rush towards a railway carriage, so sonically, for Tim Riley, does the final number where Ringo's opening tom-tom fill 'doesn't establish the beat so much as it tumbles down into it … and the effect is like jumping onto a moving train'. Riley continues that, 'When the first verse begins, it's like a whole new world opening – the music defines ecstasy' (1988: 67), and the 'She Loves You' sequence in *A Hard Day's Night* works to record that ecstasy, rapidly alternating shots of band and audience unified. The central catalyst to this communal euphoria is the refrain 'yeah, yeah, yeah' – an affirmation so synonymous with the Beatles that it became their alternative name throughout continental Europe. To this must be added the falsetto 'ooh', (adopted from the Isley Brothers), a cue for Paul and George invariably to shake their mop-tops and, as recorded in the film, consequently raise further the intensity of audience 'hysteria'. So well-known was the song and so familiar its delivery that Lester's film can largely bypass the group's performance, partly to add further sight gags – McCartney Senior rising through the trap door, the frazzled director slumped over his console – but mainly to dwell on the young (now co-starring) audience.

Before the final song starts the film shows 20 seconds of auditorium mayhem. Then, with eight separate cuts from the Beatles to the audience, the group are on screen for 63 seconds, their screaming fans for 76 seconds, including a full half-minute immediately before the final chorus. As the Beatles sing their last long 'yeah' and the fans cry out for more, we complete our vicarious experience of the new 'youthquake' through what Ian MacDonald terms 'one of the most explosive pop records ever made' (1994: 74). However, all does not remain affective abandon and empowerment. When the group take their final bow, there bursts into light behind them a large electrical sign. There is no visual play on images here as, in the film's least ambivalent moment, the sign declares in large illuminated letters 'BEATLES' (see Figure 1.4). Lest we forget, the brand name shines out at internal and external audiences. The fans are encouraged to revert to consumers, to augment their parasocial intimacy by purchasing the associated badges, tea towels, shirts, coat-hangers, Beatle-wigs, plastic models, postcards and, of course, the soundtrack album.

The phenomenon tardily labelled Beatlemania penetrated not just music and cinema but fashion, language and even a life-affirming belief system. In their debut feature, calculated examples of such an all-encompassing and exhaustively exploited youth culture may have struck the knowing George as 'grotty', but style-guru Simon was right to insist that everyone would want to buy in. And this constitutes the final, overarching duality of *A Hard Day's Night*, a film which, despite its undoubted stylistic innovations and thematic insurrections, would aggressively service hegemonic capitalist impulses. Its success meant that the influence of *A Hard Day's Night* on youth culture would prove pervasive. It changed the musical soundscape, encouraging a move towards freer expression. As Jerry Garcia from the counterculture's free-form favourites Grateful Dead recalled, 'I

Figure 1.4. A Hard Day's Night – youth culture commodified.

think the movie had more impact on me and everybody I knew than [prior Beatle] music did ... All of a sudden it seemed that the musical possibilities opened way up' (quoted in Joseph 1973: 188). Visually breaking pop music free of imitative performance in a diegetic mode, its shaping of the music video format, especially in the 'Can't Buy Me Love' sequence, is readily acknowledged. In 1984 the MTV channel (1981–present) sent Lester a vellum scroll naming him 'the father of the music video' – with a typical tongue-in-cheek undercutting of generational intolerance, Lester's reply insisted on a paternity test (Glynn 2005: 90–4). Television aped the film's musical antics in *The Monkees* (NBC, 1966–8), creating a pre-Fab Four that even bore a similarly misspelt animal name (Lefcowitz 1989: 7–8).

The Beatles' cinematic 'foreign import' also changed the style and content of American filmmaking, providing a formative template for several future-New Hollywood directors.[5] Francis Ford Coppola 'concedes that *A Hard Day's Night* ... had inspired him' on *You're A Big Boy Now* (1966), his Cannes-entered *Graduate*-pre-empting graduate thesis piece (Cowie 1989: 32–3); William Friedkin's first feature, *Good Times* (1967), was 'another attempt, like the Monkees, to rip off *A Hard Day's Night*' (Biskind 1998: 202), only replacing the Beatles *faute de mieux* with Sonny and Cher; Monkees' co-creator Bob Rafelson dismantled his clean-cut ersatz Beatles in his feature debut *Head* (1968), '*A Hard Day's Night* directed by Jean-Luc Godard rather than Richard Lester' (Greene 2008: 6). However, both Friedkin's and Rafelson's films flopped, while Coppola's countercultural calling-card led instead to directing the residual Fred Astaire vehicle *Finian's Rainbow* (1968). Clearly only one combination could successfully continue the momentum of *A Hard Day's Night* – and Lester duly returned to film the Beatles in their sophomore effort, *Help!*

Notes

1 Lennon remarked to journalist Maureen Cleave in a UK interview that 'Christianity will go. It will vanish and shrink. We're more popular than Jesus now' (1966). Republished five months later during the Beatles' third US tour, Lennon's pronouncement led to an orchestrated hate campaign with the Ku Klux Klan coming out in force and Beatles merchandise and effigies being publicly consigned to sacrificial fires. See Savage (2015: 323-9).

2 Recognising his importance in creating their suits, the Beatles insisted a cameo role be written for their 'house tailor', Dougie Millings. Millings thus appears in *A Hard Day's Night* as a frustrated tailor, unable to measure up a constantly moving Paul before John cuts his tape and, in mock-regal tones, 'declare[s] this bridge open'.

3 35 years later, the distaff world domination effected by Britain's Spice Girls would be again facilitated by a pop music film vehicle, *Spiceworld: The Movie*

(Spiers, 1997). With its fraught passage to a climactic concert performance, it proffered an open homage to the Beatles' film debut (Glynn 2013: 200-4).

4 Beatle-led female empowerment in the workplace? Alfred Aronowich reported how, in one instance, when 'a foreman shut off the radio in the middle of a Beatles record at a textile mill in Lancashire, 200 girls went out on strike' (1964: 32).

5 Robert B. Ray notes that, while it would be hard to exaggerate the Beatles' influence on US teenagers growing up in the 1960s, 'It would be harder still to exaggerate the impact that *A Hard Day's Night* had on the American film industry' (1985: 270).

2 The Beatles minus youth culture

Help! (1965)

This chapter shows how the Beatles' second film possesses stylistic continuities and further dual readings, only now with a different slant. Again utilising the prism of modernist aesthetics and pop art practices, *Help!* explores the increasingly powerful position of youth culture's primary icons but now emphasises the concomitant constraints Beatlemania had imposed on their daily lives. The Fab Four's ostensible freedoms are predicated through scenes foregrounding both international travel and the burgeoning centrality of 'Swinging London' to youth culture and its pleasures. Against this, their restrictions are allusively presented through genre parody, with the foreign cults that block the Beatles' attempts at creative expression offering a metaphorical displacement of the group's over-enthusiastic fanbase. This playful strategy is shown, nonetheless, to have problematic ideological and economic corollaries. Firstly, in spoofing British espionage narrative tropes, *Help!* also inherits such films' reactionary depictions of race and gender, an unfortunate regression from their debut film's inclusive fan portrayal. Secondly, as it begins to co-opt the iconography of Empire, *Help!* illustrates the nexus of a new and concerted British invasion, with its indigenous youth culture pointedly repackaged for global commercial consumption.

Production and reception

When their contract had been signed with United Artists, the Beatles were a relatively localised success. Now an international phenomenon with unprecedented potential, the budget for their follow-up film was doubled to (a still modest) £400,000/$1.1 million, and the shooting schedule raised from 8 to 11 weeks (23 February to 11 May). Retained were producer Walter Shenson and director Richard Lester, but elsewhere it was all change. David Watkin came in as Director of Photography for Gilbert Taylor, who withdrew, convinced by his experience on *A Hard Day's Night* that the Beatles were a baleful influence on the young (Walker 1974: 267, 269). George Martin remained as song producer, but creative differences with Lester meant film scoring passed to Ken Thorne, who had contributed incidental music to *It's Trad, Dad!*. Fellow Oscar nominee Alun Owen was also released, the Beatles, especially Lennon, having wearied of his overplayed Scouseness.

A decision was also taken early on to move from the faux-realism of *A Hard Day's Night* to an entirely fictional and now full (Eastman)color product, though one still shorn of conventional romantic ties and again permitting the Beatles to play versions of themselves. This shift meant the group could remain ahead of the pop music film competition, now slavishly aping the New Wave stylings of their debut success – cf. stable-mates Gerry and the Pacemakers in *Ferry Cross the Mersey* (Summers, 1965). It was also felt that any attempt to repeat a remotely credible 'day in the life' representation of the Beatles' increasingly hedonistic routine would inevitably entail troubles with the censors: Lennon later recalled that by now 'the Beatles' tours were like Fellini's *Satyricon* [1969]' (quoted in Wenner 1973: 84).

Despite the change of tack, it was understood that the new film would again centre on Ringo, the quartet's most committed and least criticised actor. American Marc Behm – with credits including the screwball spy-thriller *Charade* (Donen, 1963) – worked up a scenario where, extrapolating from Ringo's earlier role, the downbeat drummer was placed under more sustained attack. This was then passed on for 'Anglicising' to the screenwriter of Lester's previous film *The Knack ... and How to Get It* (1965), the Guernsey-born Charles Wood (Soderbergh 1999: 48).

It is here that the distancing of the Beatles from their sophomore film project begins. Wood conducted his research, not first-hand like Owen, but from repeatedly viewing *A Hard Day's Night*. Thus original caricatures were intensified – John now sardonic, Paul cocky, George mean and Ringo ever put-upon – while set-piece 'witticisms' were imposed on the group rather than emanating from genuine examples of their irreverent humour. With EMI, wrong-footed on *A Hard Day's Night*, having renegotiated North American soundtrack rights, United Artists became far more interventionist and, fearful of radical content alienating fans and affecting now crucial box-office margins (cf. the Monkees' later *Head*), further Goon-like surrealism was subsumed into a more mainstream storyline. To ensure its safe delivery, a team of established comic actors were now assigned major roles, notably Leo McKern, Patrick Cargill and a returning Victor Spinetti. Alongside them were Eleanor Bron and Roy Kinnear, film debutants but emergent stars of the headline-making television satire show *That Was the Week That Was* (BBC, 1962–63, NBC 1964–65). The result of this casting strategy was that, whereas *A Hard Day's Night* had been a film 'about' and starring the Beatles, their second project was, to cite the title of their second UK album, merely 'with the Beatles'. Lennon (justifiably) complained that the Beatles 'felt like extras' in their own film (Connolly 1981: 85).

Cast and crew boarded a Boeing 707 for Nassau, New Providence Island, on Monday 22 February 1965 and then, after a two-day London stop-off, flew on 13 March to the small ski resort of Obertauern in Austria. Eight days/a week later they returned to Twickenham Studios, in and around which the rest of the film was shot, plus three days (with War Office co-operation) on Salisbury Plain (Harry 1984: 29). Though able to enjoy some relaxation in the sun and snow (plus, in a far less youth-oriented move, explore potential tax havens), the Beatles were further distanced by their boredom with an extended and no longer novel film shoot and a story line that completely failed to engage their interest. Constantly high on their new discovery, marijuana aka 'pot', the group would often corpse during takes, pushing Lester to distraction and Ornstein to discuss winding up the shoot, but commercial momentum dictated that the project should continue (Beatles 2000: 169).

Whatever their deficiencies as actors, the group were now confidently prolific songwriters and, prior to the shoot, provided Lester with thirteen lucrative album-filling compositions, seven of which were selected for filming. These were slotted at regular intervals into a plot where Ringo comes into possession of a ring originating in the Eastern temple of the Goddess Kaili, unaware that its wearer will become a human sacrifice. Unable to remove the ring, he is chased around the globe by High Priest Clang (McKern) and his murderous cult followers, initially aided but later thwarted by the cult's Priestess Ahme (Bron). Also on Ringo's trail are mad scientist Professor Foot (Spinetti) and his bumbling assistant Algernon (Kinnear) who see the ring's properties as offering the chance of world domination. Eventually the ring is removed and passed around its pursuers, releasing Ahme and the Beatles from their travails. With more time now granted for editing and printing, the Beatles' second Royal Premiere took place at the London Pavilion on 29 July, again attended by Princess Margaret, and again with chaotic crowds blocking Piccadilly Circus. The film opened at 250 leading cinemas throughout the US on 11 August.

Help! was a repeat cross-media commercial sensation. Affiliated music sales were again enormous. The singles 'Ticket to Ride' and 'Help!', both pre-film 'taster' releases, were worldwide number one hits, while the soundtrack album, now released in the US and Canada on EMI's own Capital label, gained record-breaking advance orders of over one million units, topped the Billboard chart for nine weeks and exceeded two million sales in North America. The UK version, shorn of the film's instrumental numbers but including the perennial 'Yesterday', also spent nine weeks at number one, and sold a further million copies worldwide (Coryton and Murrells 1990:

119–20). These LP figures roughly equalled the returns for *A Hard Day's Night*, as did the film itself, returning close to $6 million in the States and $14 million worldwide (Denisoff and Romanowski 1991: 139). This again constituted a huge profit – but, given a now-embedded global phenomenon to market, one could argue that such parity was (relatively) disappointing, and the critical reception for *Help!* reflected an overall sense of anti-climax.

In Britain, Michael Thornton was representative in stating that 'this isn't a nose-diving flop, that's for sure. But there is nowhere in evidence the special exciting quality of *A Hard Day's Night*' (1965). Even the music press gave the film a 'thumbs down', the *NME*'s Chris Hutchins terming it 'A hundred minutes of nonsense' and asking, 'isn't this sort of stuff reserved for Saturday morning minors?' (1965). Penelope Houston noted the follow-up's sense of removal, judging it 'less a film for people who like the Beatles *au naturel*, than for people who like all the modish things the Beatles are supposed to stand for' (1965), while John Coleman resented the more palpable design on its audience: 'as contemporary as a telly-ad for petrol or fags or detergents', *Help!* was, he felt, a film where 'suddenly one realises one is being sold the Beatles' (1965).

The group themselves remained immune to criticism, but elsewhere all was fair game. Lester's trademark direction was now considered too frantic, Felix Barker resenting how 'the boys were just jostled across the screen in a scrambled blur' (1965), and Nina Hibbin complaining that 'with never a pause for breath', the 'laughter stops [and] you find yourself sinking deeper and deeper into your seat dazed, bemused, punch-drunk, defeated, limp' (1965). Patrick Gibbs attributed Lester's increasingly 'frenetic style' to a 'lack of confidence – not in his players, surely, but in his script' and suggested that Behm and Wood had provided 'a preposterous piece into which ... any old pop group might have been dropped, so little is made of the Beatles' individual qualities' (1965).[1] Even the film's higher production values were thought to detract from the boys' character, Alexander Walker not alone in finding that 'colour cushions their impact, gives their anarchy a kind of cotton-wool softness' (1965). The BFI's heavyweight film journal, again condescending to review a youth culture product, was much in accord: Peter Harcourt questioned Lester's 'apparently inexhaustible zaniness' for 'urging us too insistently to get-with-it at all costs, to be crazy, cool, superficial and detached' and found instead 'a sadness that is the result of a lack of trust in how the Beatles really are, and in their ability to create their own effect instead of having everything contrived for them by the techniques of the film' (1965: 199).

America was similarly underwhelmed, with critical comparisons now redolent less of Welles' *Citizen Kane* than his later *F For Fake* (1973). For *Time* magazine the stars' surmised play at a sustained film career was 'a failure' with 'the charm and experimental spontaneity of *A Hard Day's Night* replaced by highly professional, carefully calculated camera work and cutting, plus a story line made out of finely wrought jack-in-the-boxes': in short, 'a Beatle [*sic*] production rather than a Beatle movie' ('Chase & Superchase' 1965). Recent convert Bosley Crowther reverted to type and lamented the 'fiasco of farcical whimseys that are thrown together' in 'a clutter of mechanical gimmicks and madcap chases' with none of the earlier film's 'welcome respite [in] pace and mood', concluding that 'The boys themselves are exuberant and uninhibited in their own genial way. They just become awfully redundant and - dare I say it? – dull' (1965: 25). The boys themselves may have claimed they 'prepared for their role' by studying *Duck Soup* (McCarey, 1933) (Norman 2003: 250), but Hollis Alpert encapsulated the collective bathos, noting that 'the humor reminded me much more of the old Abbott and Costello movies than of the Marx Brothers' (1965) – the epitome of damning with faint praise.

Problematising youth culture

The reception may have been indifferent, but *Help!* has its inspired moments. Though United Artists was now seeking a more self-contained and holistic film success, by far the most achieved sections of the movie are, ironically, the album-adjunct musical numbers. 'Ticket To Ride', a lyrical and musical advance on previous fare and the first Beatles song to break the three-minute barrier, is appropriately the most inventively filmed sequence in *Help!* and can be seen as the cinematic successor to 'Can't Buy Me Love'. Here Lester again uses the Beatles' music as a non-diegetic accompaniment to action sequences and, though lacking the earlier piece's structural release, now adds a ground-breaking rhythmic montage. Entirely fashioned post-production by John Victor Smith (Lester's regular editor thereafter), the piecing together for pace and rhythm uniquely replaces any pre-arranged choreography. Pauline Kael found *Help!* Lester's 'best edited, though not necessarily best film' (1994: 221) and this editing – now adjudged historically significant in helping to mediate French New Wave editing techniques to American film-makers (Perkins and Stollery 2004: 140–1) – is best seen in the imaginative cinematic correlation for Lennon's proto-heavy metal track and its synesthetic exposition of the potentiality in electronic amplification.

When the camera zooms in on four black dots moving up the snowy mountainside then cuts, first to the Beatles hurtling down the slope on ski-bikes, then falling back into the snow, it becomes apparent that the black images on a white background, in themselves evocative of musical notation, are also being edited to fit the opening verse's lyrical movement. During the second chorus each Beatle places a ski-pole up against the camera's corner, their faces visible through the triangular segments in the pole's stand, which they spin round to the next aperture, a rhythmic and graphic edit that simulates the cinematic process itself – and again intimates, in the midst of seeming freedom, the quartet's omnipresent mediation (see Figure 2.1).

When the first verse is repeated, the skiers are accompanied in long-shot by an animation of the song's notes along a staff composed of overhead telegraph wires – a literal presentation of the Beatles and their music through cartoon strokes. Individual shots then enact their caricatured depictions: Paul skis seriously, trying to get it right; John descends comically, making exaggerated, Goon-ish arm movements; George glides effortlessly, the image ever cool; Ringo clownishly gropes on the ground then slowly slips backwards. The next verse modulates the mise-en-scène of their debut feature by putting the boys back on a train, now as its sole occupants, a prelude to their picnicking on the snow in splendid isolation. While conveying a sense of light-headed liberty, the contrast with their earlier film's claustrophobic footage foregrounds the passage's (wishful) fantasy. As the song's final kicker fades, the quartet again descend the slope on their ski-bikes, now moving away from the camera, leaving behind a scene of improvised and unskilled fun – though one meticulously and skilfully edited. Textually the Beatles go back to the constraints of narrative. Contextually, though, the number takes them forward, to their own non-diegetic promotional clips – a scene of Paul on horseback will be reprised in the promotional film for 'Penny Lane' (Goldmann, 1967) – and thereafter into the ubiquitous

Figure 2.1. Help! – pop music meta-cinema.

industrial flow of television channels' storyboard music videos (Frontani 2007: 132–3).

While the 'Ticket to Ride' sequence utilises a familiar Beatles palette of black on white, elsewhere *Help!* luxuriates in its new colour medium.[2] This aesthetic shift is narratively foregrounded when, after the film's surprise, celebrity-shorn opening in Kaili's Eastern temple, the Beatles begin the title song with a return to the monochrome stylisation of *A Hard Day's Night*. Uncertainty as to how these contrasting discourses will be unified is exacerbated as Ringo is hit in the eye by a coloured dart, but fails to react. A cutback reveals a screen within a screen, the projected musical footage being attacked by an outraged Clang in his sacrificial chamber. As further darts hit their target, the opening credits spring into colourful existence, distracting attention from the Beatles and their black-and-white visual correlation. Unwittingly perhaps, the scene exposes how, with Wood's script and the Beatles' boredom, we will continue to experience the group as if at a second remove. And yet – doubleness again – in many ways this overlaid fiction will more accurately represent the group and their position in the youth culture they were accelerating than had the faux-documentary stylings of *A Hard Day's Night*. The opening of *Help!* sets up the film's epistemological core, indicative of how it will explore the differences between appearance and reality, how often seeing is deceiving.

This aspect is consummately continued in the next scene, where the four Beatles simultaneously walk up separate paths to their four individual houses, the type of modest two-storey terraced buildings ubiquitous in the northern working-class topography of British New Wave cinema (though shot in south-west London). Across the street two middle-aged women wave and comment on the boys' charms: 'lovely lads and so natural' notes the first (Gretchen Franklin), 'I mean, adoration hasn't gone to their heads one jot, has it?' Her partner (Dandy Nicholls) agrees: 'so natural, and still the same as they was before they was'. Thus we have the external image of the Beatles – essentially unchanged, the (literal) 'boy(s) next door' still rooted in a humble working-class(-ish) culture and environment. But as the quartet open each front door, a cut to inside reveals how these houses have been completely transformed, run together into one huge palatial living-space replete with state-of-the-art gadgets, automatic machines and even, for John, a sunken bed. At the time Peter Harcourt saw this as 'a world of complete fantasy … the world of Richard Lester' (1965: 199), but it can now be viewed as 'in reality' closer to the new world being experienced by the Beatles who, as Charlie Gillett notes, 'ultimately settled for what they first pulled faces at, the luxuries of the wealthy'. Though Gillett adds an acknowledgement that the group 'lightly mocked themselves as they sang' (1983: 312), the rider is here debatable, for while the Beatles clearly mocked themselves as they filmed, this is far less true of their soundtrack songs.

These numbers, as Bob Neaverson notes, convey a newly 'serious, confessional and mature tone' (1997: 41). This is most notable in Lennon's titular and lost cry for 'Help!', their first number entirely to eschew the love song formula, and (again deceptively) evidencing a lyrical poignancy behind the upbeat tempo and delivery. For Tim Riley the song's final nasal 'nnn', more repressive than a mop-top 'ooh', closes up the plaintive and elongated 'please help me' phrase 'with successively darkened tones, entrapping John's futile cries the way a movie screen freezes a frame and fades to blackness' (1988: 140). If so, presenting the number on a monochrome screen-within-a-screen provides an appropriate correlation.

Stylistically, that opening credit sequence presages the refusal of a conventional star-image presentation as, throughout the film, Lester obscures the Beatles' faces, distorts the focus or lighting, and regularly marginalises the quartet or shoots them from behind. Even when shot face-on, their confrontational stares straight into the camera now defy rather than welcome the audience's objectifying gaze. Generically, the opening further signifies how the 'fantastical' plot will supersede any 'realism' of performance. There will be fewer diegetic numbers than in *A Hard Day's Night*, none in a concert setting, and none devoid of plot interference as the pattern established in the opening track is constantly repeated. Indeed, the narrative of *Help!* constitutes a reiterated attempt to prevent the Beatles from performing. In their first film, Paul's grandfather rising through the stage trapdoor could not impede the ecstatic concert climax of 'She Loves You'. Here, however, as they serenade Ahme with 'You've Got to Hide Your Love Away', Clang's head emerges from a manhole to more obstructive effect. Army-protected performances on Salisbury Plain of 'I Need You' and 'The Night Before' are halted by underground explosions and a farcical pitched battle. Even the film's non-diegetic instrumentation moves away from the group's songs to include classical music extracts ranging from Beethoven's 'Ode to Joy', through Rossini and Tchaikovsky, to Wagner's 'Lohengrin'. As Neil Sinyard comments, 'the authentic voice of the Beatles is finding it difficult to make itself heard – which is the point' (2010: 46).

In a further instance of distanciation, that 'authentic voice' is most colourfully (if again not completely) conveyed in a venue ostensibly cocooned from the fanbase so integral to *A Hard Day's Night*. The second song sequence in *Help!*, (perhaps aptly) titled 'You're Gonna Lose That Girl', removes the Beatles to what, in real life, was increasingly becoming their preferred location – the relative privacy of the recording studio (but filmed in a mock-up at Twickenham). While initially foregrounding the mechanics of music recording – a process later extrapolated to absurdist lengths on

Salisbury Plain – and establishing spatial arrangements that (comfortingly) replicate the Beatles' live performances with George and Paul sharing one mike with John alone at another (see Figure 2.2), the overriding feature of the sequence is a series of colour filters that create a quasi-abstract choreography. This consists of blurring George and Paul in blue, balancing John screen right with a left-side slab of pink, staying with pink for close-ups of George and Paul before ending on John, where a shaft of pink shines through the blue until the light whites him out – the conclusion to a sequence of consummately achieved chromatic display.

Further undermining any documentary pretensions, during the number Ringo momentarily appears on bongos, while narrative again seems to defeat musical presentation with the revelation that the take has been ruined by Clang's gang sawing through the floor around the drummer. Nonetheless, the diffused lighting lingers on the senses beyond any destructive buzzing, and the film's first play of montage to music provides a striking visual patterning for the mise-en-scène, boldly labelled by Steven Soderbergh as 'the birth … of modern colour photography' (1999: 56).

This pioneering use of colour, be it through studio filters or location shooting – 'Another Girl', for instance, is naturalistically filmed in warm coastal shades of blue, pink and yellow on Balmoral Island – works to accentuate the film's rich visual composition. On its release Lester offered a 'soundbite' summary of *Help!* as 'Wilkie Collins' *The Moonstone* as drawn by Jasper Johns' (French 1965: 10). The similarities of the 1960s film to the 1860s novel are clear, with *Help!* presenting an energetic collaged variant

Figure 2.2. Help! – colour and comfort.

on Collins' epistolary tale of a stolen jewel being retrieved by the guardians of its Indian shrine. The comparison to American artist Jasper Johns is more contentious,[3] but validates an exploration of how Lester's film, like Johns' pop art paintings, revisits 'found images' and makes viewers 'think about representation and the paradoxes it entails' (Hughes 1991: 340).

For instance, much as a Johns piece such as *0 through 9* (1961) revealed a tension between recognisable signifiers and the shapes' abstract quality, the successive titles in *Help!* enumerating five attempts to steal Ringo's ring work cognitively and generatively to provide secure and predictable containers for the chaotic action initiated therein. Johns constantly revisited the Stars and Stripes, as with *White Flag* (1955) where, Robert Hughes notes, 'we see the painting first, that pale, perfect skin; but the flag beneath it, the sign, has lost its power to command' (1991: 341). Flags feature constantly, and with equal impotence, in *Help!*, as when the Union Jack sported by the swimmer (Mal Evans) emerges from the Alpine ice, as lost as Britain in its post-Suez geo-political disorientation, as disorientated as the Beatles themselves in their global goldfish bowl.

Echoes of other pop artists can also be found in *Help!*'s brightly patterned bitter-sweet projections. The film, like its predecessor, again resonates strongly with the practices of Andy Warhol, who would 'create an art that was popular, mass-produced, aimed at youth, witty, sexy, gimmicky, glamorous and Big Business, but he would also deal with hero-worship, religious hogwash, the banality inherent to modern materialism, world-weariness' (Shanes 2009: 18). Amidst the closing credits' vertiginous multiplication of images in the cut glass of the plot-motivating red ring, we view, akin to the Warhol canvas – taken from *Flaming Star* (Siegel, 1960) – of a gun-slinging *Triple Elvis* (1962), an unarmed triple Paul. The star's form is once more pushed towards abstraction yet also rendered a product for consumption, uncomfortably like the film-profligate Presley. Right to the end, as John Coleman's review noted, here are the Beatles for Sale.

Closer to home, the work of Britain's Peter Phillips is similarly ambivalent, conveying 'the excitement he felt as a young man when confronted by the signs of the new teenage culture' though with 'disquieting overtones evident even in these exuberant works' (Livingstone 2000: 153). A Phillips piece such as *Purple Flag* (1960) combines imagery prevalent both in Johns and Lester, while *War/Game* (1961) yokes together flags, military uniforms and slabs of colour, all similarly central to the visual style of *Help!*. In vogue and exhibited as part of 'The New Generation' at London's Whitechapel Gallery in 1964, Phillips described his colourful paintings as 'multi-assemblages of special, iconographical and technical factors which combine to make one object' (Various 1964: 72) – the same holds for Lester's contemporaneous first colour movie.

Help! not only continues Lester's auteurist adaptation of contemporary art practices, but also retains his ludic quotations from cinema itself. The plethora of pratfalls and sight gags again foreground silent cinema practice, while intertitles and the play with graphic data recall the modernist aesthetics of Jean-Luc Godard. These allusions may work as 'in jokes' for older film critics or even add a fan service for more cine-literate young viewers, but *Help!* is more intertextually accessible to its core audience by employing the codes and conventions of the on-trend espionage film genre, specifically the Beatles' (and United Artists') partner in international success, James Bond. The plot line of *Help!* is reminiscent of the already formulaic narratives encountered in *Dr. No* (Young, 1962) and *Goldfinger* (Hamilton, 1964), with various attempts on the hero's life prompting set-piece chases and high definition colour photography through Antillaise and Alpine scenery. Parody abounds, especially with *Goldfinger*: dousing Ringo in red house paint evokes the 'skin-suffocating' gold spray punitively applied to Jill Masterson (Shirley Eaton); Foot's mad scientist redeploys Auric Goldfinger (Gert Fröbe)'s industrial laser to burn through Ringo's flesh – if only he can find a working plug. The play with subterfuge also furthers *Help!*'s epistemological imperative, as when Ahme informs us, straight to camera, that 'I am not what I seem'. And the Beatles? As they stroll uncommitted through the irony and allusions, one could (just) claim that Bond's personal characteristics are divided amongst them, with Paul the seducer of women, John and George sharing the acerbic wit and fighting prowess (John deadly with a lamp-shade, George fearless with a glue-brush), and poor Ringo the constantly endangered protagonist.[4] The character distinction, though, so important to *A Hard Day's Night*, is here culturally diluted, a favour to neither young nor old.

Another disadvantage of *Help!*'s spy-inspired doubleness – satirising the competing Bond film cycle while simultaneously employing its narrative and visual formulae – is that the film also inherits the Bond films' less youth cultural and more reactionary ideology. I have elsewhere examined in detail the perils of such a parodic approach, especially in *Help!*'s depiction of race and gender relationships, which has significantly contributed to the film's failure to remain as affectionately in the public consciousness as its predecessor (Glynn 2011). This disquietude only intensifies if one moves beyond the hermetic sphere of cinematic intertextuality to explore how closely *Help!* relates to the real-life experiences of those youth icons, the Beatles themselves.

The prescience of *Help!* at both surface and profound levels has been regularly noted – Neil Sinyard terms it 'an uncommonly prophetic film' and, like Lester (quoted in di Franco 1978: 23), points out how the group's hirsute airport disguises 'might have looked grotesque and unlikely at the time, but, in five years, some of the Beatles are actually going to look like that' (2010: 45) – cf. *Let It Be*. One could add another visual indicator, with the boys briefly glimpsed in military band attire celebrating Clang's ski descent, a foretaste of the merger of Victorian and Edwardian regimental jackets that would form the fashion base for *Sgt. Pepper's Lonely Hearts Club Band* and mid-1960s Carnaby Street. At a more foundational level, the Beatles' position as targets for religious zealots vaguely apprehends the summer 1966 US backlash that would follow Lennon's 'bigger than Jesus' comparison, and even his Dakota shooting by Mark Chapman on 8 December 1980, a landmark event dramatised in both *The Killing of John Lennon* (Piddington, 2006) and *Chapter 27* (Schaefer, 2007).

Further still, the blood-letting sacrifices ensconced in the group's cartoonish adventure faintly foreshadow the 8–9 August 1969 Hollywood murders by Beatle-obsessive Charles Manson and his Family followers, an industry tipping-point explored/exploited with a more visceral (but arguably equally belaboured) violence in the alternative-history ending to *Once Upon a Time... in Hollywood* (Tarantino, 2019). Mostly, though, the film's *Moonstone* mockery seems premonitory of Eastern cultural influences on the group's more peaceful countercultural musical soundscapes, men's fashion and mental outlook. The origins of this personal development can be traced back to the filming of *Help!* when, shooting the 'Rajahama' Indian restaurant scenes at Twickenham, George first encountered musicians playing the sitar, had a copy made of the Indian jacket with stand collar worn by Clang and Co. (designed by Julie Harris), while in the Bahamas a genuine Swami (Vishnu Devananda) gave him a copy of *The Illustrated Book of Yoga* (Beatles 2000: 171) – future help for Beatles whose independence had seemed to 'vanish in the haze'.

Retreating from such potentially infinite projections, however, *Help!* can be cogently seen as demonstrating, though displaced into allegorical form, the contemporary situation of the Beatles and their shifting relationship to the youth culture they had advanced. As Devin McKinney notes, the film serves as 'a comic strip of what the Beatles' real lives were becoming' (2003: 72). Here we can witness an intensification of themes rendered more implicitly in *A Hard Day's Night*, where the Beatles' cheerful acceptance helped to play down their followers' attendant oppressiveness and the latent threat to their well-being. Nonetheless, the signs were there and, if one can block out the innovation and ebullience, their debut film's opening train escape reveals the group's scant personal respite. On leaving the platform, the shot from inside the Beatles' compartment is of screaming fans and the unremitting click of camera flashes. Their first song performance has them framed cage-like in the luggage compartment, while a minor but potentially telling detail has Ringo jerk his head away from stretched out, clawing schoolgirl fingers. When they reach their hotel room, they remain prisoners of their celebrity, forced by manager Norm to stay in and answer fan mail.

Lester has referenced John's appraisal of the group's October 1963 visit to Sweden as 'a room and a car and a car and a room and a concert' and building the early sequences of *A Hard Day's Night* around this feeling of enclosed spaces: 'prisoners in space, prisoners of fans, prisoners by car, train, small hotel rooms – do this, do that, sign this' (quoted in di Franco 1978: 5). Tactfully, though, John's real-life complaint about restrictive tour practices was instead placed, almost verbatim, into the mouth of Paul's fictional grandfather, an astute strategy, since its attribution to any Beatle could have conveyed an alienating sense of ingratitude. Instead the older generation's crotchety evaluation of the indefatigably upbeat group's daily grind allows the viewer to sympathise by proxy with the Fab Four.

Help!'s metaphorical before mimetic depictions allow an (admittedly coded) shedding of such reticence and the sense of threat is instead amplified in a madcap plot where, now protected from invasive hordes by the British Army rather than lines of police officers, the Beatles are nonetheless blown up, blowtorched, defenestrated, drowned, encaged, electrocuted, fired upon and operated on, pierced, prodded and shrunk. However, the tonal leavening this time comes from more strained smile-inducing quips and/or more melancholy foot-tapping song accompaniments. Concomitant with this shift to exaggerated exotic adventure, the female fans, so powerful and persistent a presence in *A Hard Day's Night*, are here numerically paltry and narratively passive. Ahme, though a principal character, quickly defers to the male heroes, betraying her own religious quest in return for an affectionate wink from Paul. Elsewhere (beyond the tentative – and older – couple watching the Beatles come home) the female is completely silent, a decorative commodity reified to the extent that, while the other Beatles swap instruments, 'ladies-man' Paul can use a bikini-clad actress as a bass guitar substitute to 'play on' as he sings of taking what he wants and getting yet 'Another Girl' (see Figure 2.3). In its fantasy setting the group can disembark at Nassau International Airport free of screaming, banner-waving fans and even enter the City Barge pub in London to order drinks without the barmaid recognising them.

That last location is important since, for all its overseas travel, *Help!* is anchored in the world's new capital of youth culture. As the chased Beatles ski straight into the Alpine railway ticket-office, John cathartically cries out the globally 'with it' destination of 'London!' Present thereafter are all the images necessary for international recognition: Buckingham Palace, the Coldstream Guards, Carnaby Street fashions – and, of course, the Beatles themselves. *Help!* is, as described by Philip Norman, 'Swinging London personified – part-music, part colour-supplement travelogue, part-Pop Art strip cartoon' (2003: 249). Diegetically, though, this new cultural capital and its denizens are (again) not uniformly accepted,

Figure 2.3. Help! – the Beatles' *Bikini Beach.*

notably by Scotland Yard's superintendent (the older generation equivalent of *A Hard Day's Night*'s train commuter) who – mistakenly – informs
John that 'you won't last, you know'. However, the major threats emerge
less from the Establishment – the Beatles receive refuge in the mon-
arch's Westminster residence – than from Britain's technological future
and imperial past. When Professor Foot's 'relativity cadenza' reduces the
Beatles to slow-motion action, it figuratively demonstrates how, in addition to their female fanbase, the increasingly close attentions of the intellectual classes (Lennon's later 'expert texperts') were already starting to
cramp the Beatles' style, to spoil the youthful fun.

The depiction of Britain's technocracy remains disarming, though,
principally because of its self-deprecation. Foot is ever-frustrated by the
(perceived) lack of government funding: failing detonators are 'ex-Army
rubbish: I can't get the equipment!' His assistant's incompetence draws a
diatribe on Harold Wilson's planned 'democratisation' of UK education via
the distance-learning Open University: 'That's what comes from teaching
science by television!'

Far less appealing, however, are the film's depictions of the British Empire
striking back. In a further (and distasteful) act of distanciation, both Clang's
cohort, a parody of the Indian Thuggee cult, and the Indian restaurant staff
where the Beatles seek guidance, are all played by white Western actors,
and the culture they portray is deliberately – and derogatorily – played for

laughs. For instance, when Bhuta (John Bluthal) hears Clang talking on the underground, he shrugs his shoulders and declares: 'I don't speak the language, you see. Latin, yes, but this Eastern babble?' Ahme too promises John that she is not using her 'filthy Eastern ways'. Add in 'one from the sunnier clime, East of Suez' in the restaurant's coal-hole, running to a bed of nails at the sight of Ringo's ring, plus the finale's white-jacketed, quick-marching West Indian police officers obediently helping their UK overlords to defeat the Kaili cultists, and throughout the film one witnesses only crude stereotypes of a mystic East and compliant Caribbean. These are examples of what Jim Pines terms 'one of the characteristics of colonial and main-stream race-relations discourses' where 'the colonised subject does not have access to the means of self-representation'. Thus, just like *Help!*'s female characters, they lack an 'active voice' (2008: 121).

This is doubly disconcerting if one interprets *Help!*, distinct from its predecessor in ostensibly eliminating Beatlemania, as allegorically trans-ferring that claustrophobic presence onto the more overtly antagonistic Eastern cult demanding Ringo's sacrifice. Narratively, Clang and Co. take the place of the Beatles' fanbase in constantly interrupting the group's per-formances and assailing their persons. Furthermore, their revered Goddess Kaili, the 'killer of demons' bracketing the film in her giant, multi-armed effigy form, symbolically 'represent[s] the shadow of the Female over the Beatles' (McKinney 2003: 78), i.e. that youthful audience with its many-fingered increasingly invasive threat.

It is, in all aspects, a regrettable transposition. Eugenia Paulicelli and Louise Wallenberg have noted how the documentary *The Beatles: Eight Days a Week - The Touring Years* (Howard, 2016) – an honorary adjunct to the Beatles' filmography in testifying to 'the unprecedented impact youth and popular culture had in the development of new ways of behaving and interacting in public and private, dressing, thinking, and consuming in the early and mid-1960s' – offers fresh

> insights into how Beatlemania and live concerts offered opportunities and space for young people to express their rebellion against old hier-archies of class, generation and race. Not only whites were enthusias-tic about the Beatles, but also African Americans, Asians, and people across the globe.
>
> (2017: 3)

Howard's documentary also highlights the group's refusal to play at the Gator Bowl in Jacksonville, Florida (11 September 1964) if the audience remained racially segregated, a clear sign of support for the US civil rights movement. What a shame, therefore, that such fans, elsewhere empowered by their encounters with the Beatles on tour and their inclusive multiracial soundtrack,[5] should see in *Help!* such negative screen depictions of black, Asian and minority ethnicities.

As with the science and technology strand, though, an argument could be advanced in the film's defence that it offers more wittingly reductive depictions of Britain's own traditional heroism, military might and religious rites. The stiff-upper-lipped altruism of Britain's past is invoked by Paul's reference to Antarctic explorer Lawrence 'Titus' Oates when he muses to Ringo: 'That bloke with Scott, I always admired the way he went out into the snow for his mates'. Ringo, though, will not replicate such actions: the noble age of self-sacrifice is over. The Salisbury Plain numbers show the full weight of Britain's military hardware struggling to protect the Beatles from piecemeal foreign attacks. An aerial shot, repeating the opening visual patterning in Kaili's temple by placing the group inside a circle of 3rd Division Centurion tanks, equates Eastern religion and the Western war machine via the mise-en-scène. The trope is repeated during the 'I Need You' sequence when a close-up of the neck of George's trusted Gibson J-160E precedes a refocus which reveals in long-shot the ancient landmark of Stonehenge and renders the guitar's frets as large on screen as the monument's standing stones. Narratively, the presence of Stonehenge offers a reminder that sacrificial ceremonies are not the sole preserve of alien cultures. Contextually, the shift intuits, as with the helicopter ending to *A Hard Day's Night*, how the Beatles are the new focus of a nation's worship, and one, for all the frantic plot's attendant hardware, advocating love, not war.

Help!'s belittling of the agents of Imperialism was compromised, however, when, between the film's wrap and release, came the 12 June announcement that the Labour government's Queen's Honours List had awarded each Beatle an MBE – the Most Excellent Order of the British Empire. The news stirred up strong national feelings. Lennon's mild sarcasm, 'I thought you had to drive tanks and win wars to get an MBE', would be undermined by his role in the battle-strewn hipness of *Help!*. Meanwhile several real-life equivalents of *A Hard Day's Night*'s commuter and *Help!*'s superintendent returned their medals 'in protest that an honour hard won through War or subpostmastership should be given to what one outraged Naval hero described as "a gang of nincompoops"' (Norman 2003: 248, 251). Again mistakenly – these societal pillars did not see how the award was, at least initially, very much a victory for their older generation. Just as the Beatles were implicitly rejecting the attentions of their fanbase, here was an openly recuperative coup by a white-haired pipe-smoking Prime Minister showing himself in tune with, and on top of, the values of the young.

Harold Wilson's vote-seeking award was ostensibly in recognition of the Beatles' export potency, their position at the vanguard of a worldwide purchasing of product from a Britain currently mired in debt. Arguably this is where, for all its differences and disappointments, *Help!* ultimately continues and consolidates the cinematic achievements of *A Hard Day's Night*. While the Indian Empire and British Army authority were long gone and therefore easy targets for ex-Lancer Charles Wood's satire, in their place had arisen a newly authoritative empire – that of Youth Culture. For a brief shining moment the Beatles spearheaded an ethos and aesthetic, centred on 'Swinging London', that created systems of demand for and consumption of British goods amongst freshly dependent international markets. Here, replacing the now-mocked geo-political, was a glorified neo-Elizabethan age of British *cultural* imperialism. Pushed by the increasingly globalised operations of EMI, the Beatles were the most pervasive image of this 'British invasion', with *Help!* in all its iterations extending the penetrative work of its predecessor in displacing indigenous products and disseminating UK values and practices in countries as far apart as Argentina and New Zealand. The US became so alarmed at this reversal of pop fortunes that its Labour Department tried to ban British acts from entering the country, but the Beatles were far too lucrative to be included in such panic-driven protectionism and, with the necessary palms greased, the group returned to America on 13 August to promote their new film and soundtrack album. Thus, for all its Eastern imagery and lyrical introspection, the Beatles' second film ultimately constituted the dissemination of ideologies fully consonant with bullish western capitalism. Significantly, the two most achieved sections of *Help!*, the 'so natural' Beatles returning to their *trompe l'oeil* terrace-row housing and relaxing as tourists at an Alpine ski resort, not only indicate the boys retreating from their public but also privately comfortable with the benefits of capital.

Help!, a tonally uncertain film, captures the Beatles, both for personal expression and public exposure, at an indeterminate stage in their career. Metaphorically battling against both their youth fanbase in the guise of the Eastern cultists and the older intelligentsia in the person of the scientists, the film, as Stephanie Fremaux notes, comments on the Beatles being 'stuck in the middle of two groups vying for the band's attention' (2018: 50). At the time, Peter Harcourt felt that the Beatles, rather like Lester's characters in *The Knack*, 'inhabit that no-man's-land of adolescent get-with-it-ness, that formerly awkward age which exists between sexual awareness and sexual experience' and deduced that 'it could be commercially disastrous if the Beatles were allowed to change and grow up' (1965: 199). Nonetheless, the liminal spaces and lukewarm reception of *Help!* showed that the Beatles were no longer at home in the youth cultural moment globally experienced as Beatlemania. Change and grow up they had to, their maturation leading them to the less commercial and unchartered territory of their more adult preoccupations and, if not quite the disaster Harcourt predicted, the new experience of a relative film failure – roll up for the *Magical Mystery Tour* and the wider counterculture.

Notes

1 As if to prove his statement on the Beatles' loss of individuality, Gibbs mistakenly labels a miniaturised Beatle as John, not Paul.
2 The tagline on American publicity posters emphasised *Help!*'s chromatic promise: 'The Colorful Adventures of THE BEATLES are more colorful than ever ... in COLOR!'
3 Lester later distanced himself from any explicit influence by Johns: 'it was just a means to explain it' (quoted in Soderbergh 1999: 49).
4 Bond got his retaliation in first (but exposed his 'square' sensibility), remarking to Jill Masterson in *Goldfinger* that 'My dear girl, there are some things that just aren't done, such as drinking Dom Perignon '53 above the temperature of 38 degrees Fahrenheit. That's just as bad as listening to the Beatles without earmuffs!'
5 Ian MacDonald emphasises how, especially with the influence of doo-wop and Tamla Motown records on their compositions, 'the Beatles acted as a major conduit of black energy, style and feeling into white culture' (1994: 9).

3   The Beatles and the counterculture

Magical Mystery Tour (1967) and *Yellow Submarine* (1968)

This chapter explores, through their film work, the Beatles' shift into the 1960s counterculture. A youth movement whose core values present a challenge to the dominant, adult culture, counterculture is a broad descriptor obscuring numerous divisions. Often equated with hippiedom and its attendant psychedelia that originated on America's West Coast before spreading across the US, Western Europe and even the Eastern bloc, its British variant was rather different. While equally influenced by the beats' artistic intelligentsia and the liberal humanitarianism of the CND movement, it was nonetheless (lengthily) devoid of explicit political orientation, seeking to create an alternative yet inclusive way of life, espousing love and freedom of expression. There was no single blueprint for this. Some 'turned on' to consciousness-expanding substances, notably LSD and/or cannabis, 'by far the most important drug of the new youth culture' (Leech 1976: 38). Others 'tuned in' to new aesthetic experiences and different media, evident in the UK flowering of an underground press such as *Oz* that explored form as much as content, plus arts centres and venues such as London's Roundhouse which conducted large-scale musical happenings where 'anything went' (Wheen 1982: 162). Some 'dropped out', pursuing utopian ideals through the communal good life – an option indicative of this youth movement's more middle-class origins (Clarke et al. 1976: 60–1). Each approach is signalled in the two Beatles films of this period which, though receiving very different popular and critical responses, both presented hallucinogenic and/ or meditative 'trips', employed a plethora of multimedia arts practices, and blended prior communal activities, be it Blackpool coach-trips or Edwardian bandstands, into new youth/countercultural hybrids. As with other subcultures, though, the values of the counterculture were recuperated, and their articulation, as evidenced here, was transformed into a branch of popular entertainment: even the counterculture was swiftly monetised.

This new direction took time to find a group film expression. *Help!* had, narratively and structurally, revealed the Beatles' growing preference for working in the recording studio – a focus that would culminate in the richly-textured album *Rubber Soul* (December 1965), the proto-psychedelic *Revolver* (August 1966) and the soundtrack for the Summer of Love, *Sgt. Pepper's Lonely Hearts Club Band* (May 1967). The concert fatigue that led to the group quitting live performances after 29 August 1966 at Candlestick Park is fully evident in the documentary *Eight Days a Week: The Touring Years*, but they were now equally unwilling to spend months hanging around a film lot, and thus several proposals for their contracted third film venture were summarily dismissed. The group vetoed Walter Shenson's offer to appear in an adaptation of Richard Condon's 1871-set comedy western novel *A Talent for Loving*. They also rejected the chance to star in a comic adaptation of Alexandre Dumas' *The Three Musketeers*, despite the prospect of Richard Lester again directing and the mooted casting as Lady de Winter of Brigitte Bardot, an obsession for Lennon since *Doctor at Sea* (Thomas, 1955), her first English-language film (Norman 2008: 73). With increasing exasperation, Lennon in particular vehemently objected to Epstein's negotiated involvement in Walt Disney's *The Jungle Book* (1967) – though their proposed cameo remained as a mop-topped quartet of vultures, now with cod-Scouse accents and a song more barbershop than British beat.

With the absence of touring now opening out their previously packed schedule, film discussions would in time be held with nouvelle vague iconoclast Jean–Luc Godard, not least known for shooting his projects quickly (O'Dell 2002: 119–20), with Patrick McGoohan, whose surreal television series *The Prisoner* (ITV, 1967–68) the Beatles greatly admired, and with playwright David Halliwell for his prescient student-protest comedy *Little Malcolm and his Struggle Against the Eunuchs*, but none came to fruition (Beatles 2000: 272).[1] While potentially more in line with the group's desired move from 'youth' towards a more adult 'culture', even the possibility of Michelangelo Antonioni directing failed to coax them towards Owen Holder's experimental screenplay *Shades of A Personality*.[2] Shenson, however, was convinced the split-personality project had promise and commissioned a 'punched-up' rewrite from the West End's new *enfant terrible* Joe Orton – a positive 24 January 1967 meeting with McCartney at Brian Epstein's Belgravia house was recreated in the Orton biopic *Prick Up Your Ears* (Frears, 1987).

Orton's radically reworked version, retitled *Up Against It*, had the boys 'caught in flagrante, become involved in dubious political activity, dressed as women, committed murder, been put in prison and committed adultery' (Lahr 1986: 83). His proffered script was, after a lengthy delay, returned without comment – thus provoking plentiful speculation. Was the anarchic content just too much too soon for the self-proclaimed newly progressive Beatles? Orton certainly thought so: 'I gather that the script wasn't conventional enough', he diplomatically told the press ('A Hard Day's Hunt' 1967) – 'fuck them', he noted more demotically in his diary (4 April) (Lahr 1986: 130). Revealing a progressive retrenchment in their cinematic depictions of gender and sexuality, McCartney later claimed it was the explicit queer politics – what Orton termed the 'opportunities for sexual ambiguities' (Lahr 1986: 64) – that had put them off: 'it wasn't that we were anti-gay – it's just that we, the Beatles, weren't gay' (Carr 1996: 135). More pragmatically, Lester (who picked up the script as a potential vehicle for Mick Jagger) had felt its verbal dexterity and discipline was evidently beyond their acting reach (Yule 1994: 166–8).

All were no doubt contributory factors. Above all, though, the Beatles were by now seeking greater self-determination, knowing they did *not* want to be obligated to the annual film drudgery and blandness endured by former idol Elvis Presley. This was far from an aversion to film itself and the medium's possibilities for artistic expression, as evidenced, amidst abortive group discussions, by their concurrent solo cinematic ventures, a range of experience and exposure that problematises Ian MacDonald's view that at this juncture the Beatles 'wandered, drug-dozy, into the medium of film, assuming that anyone with a few ideas could turn out something watchable' (1994: 224).[3] Rather, Kenneth Womack's interpretation of the Beatles' musical output as an 'act of life-writing' whereby they 'engaged in a self-conscious effort to tell their own stories about the inherent difficulties that come with growing up and growing older', can also be applied to their increasingly self-selected film work (2010: 262).

Lennon reunited with Lester in Almería, Spain (in autumn 1966) for a brief role as Musketeer Gripweed in the Second World War-set black comedy *How I Won the War* (October 1967) – and definitively severed his mop-top connections by cutting his hair and adopting his henceforth trademark round 'granny glasses'. The ever-adventurous McCartney, who scored the X-certificated comedy-drama *The Family Way* (Boulting, 1966), had also started experimenting with sound and Super-8 film footage, as in (lost) avant-garde home movies such as *The Defeat of the Dog* and *The Next Spring Then*, reputedly shown to Antonioni when in London filming *Blow Up* (Miles 1997: 296–301). Starr, (in August 1967) offered the cameo role of Mexican gardener Emmanuel in United Artists' psychedelic porn satire *Candy* (Marquand, 1968), had pursued his interest in photography and become a keen collector and exponent of cameras and colour filters (Clayson 2003: 167).[4] Harrison, increasingly frustrated in his songwriting opportunities, would willingly accept the (late-1967) invite from director Joe Massot to compose the soundtrack for his sensory and voyeuristic *Wonderwall* (1968) – the resultant Anglo-Indian *Wonderwall Music* became the first LP released on the Beatles' self-operated Apple Records (Inglis

2010: 16–18). All these discrete musical and cinematic interests would cohere in the Beatles' first project following Brian Epstein's overdose demise on 27 August 1967, the self-financed, self-produced, self-directed, self-written, self-scored and self-starring *Magical Mystery Tour*, a 52-minute special brokered late in proceedings for BBC television.

Magical Mystery Tour – televised counterculture's rejection

Celebrity-led specials were a regular feature of the television schedules throughout the 1960s (and 1970s) and this semi-improvised project, conceived by McCartney back in April 1967, was a Beatle-led strategy not only to retain group unity in the post-Epstein vacuum but also, keeping ahead of the competition, to 'gatecrash the medium and do something unusual at the same time' (Ingham 2006: 198). Denis O'Dell, assistant producer on *A Hard Day's Night*, was brought in to help the group with production duties and the embryonic 'skrupt', an eight-section pie-chart written out by Paul on a single sheet of A4, was realised with a budget of £30,000/$85,000 (Neaverson 1997: 47). *Magical Mystery Tour* is often seen as a West Country variant on the 1964 psychedelic-painted bus journey by Ken Kesey and his Merry Pranksters – a drug-fuelled counterculture 'trip' across America that included playing the *Help!* album at full volume through the vehicle's external speakers (Wolfe 1989 [1968]: 179–80). However, it is also recognisable as a traditional Northern British working-class coach outing (familiar to industrial employees in the era before mass car ownership). As George later clarified, 'It was basically a charabanc trip, which people used to go on from Liverpool to see the Blackpool lights – they'd get loads of crates of beer and all get pissed' (Beatles 2000: 272).

This 'piss-up' took two weeks to film. The Beatles, together with a skeleton crew and a cast of passengers drawn from friends, fans and jobbing actors intuitively selected from the *Spotlight* directory, headed off not north but across south-west England on 11 September 1967 before convening (for want of having booked studio space) at the disused Hangar No 2 of West Malling Air Station in Maidstone, Kent. The filming style matched the content's grafting of an LA hippie commune onto Lancashire holiday customs. The influence of Dadaism and Surrealism is regularly highlighted (Reiter 2008: 106) but, as Stephanie Fremaux points out, to ground their trip in an authenticating realism, 'the band employs an unscripted, handheld camera style reminiscent of Lester's cinema vérité in *A Hard Day's Night*' (2018: 86). Editing down the ten hours of footage under the supervision of Roy Benson (previously part of John Jympson's team on *A Hard Day's Night*), and completing the soundtrack with George Martin at Abbey Road, took a further eleven weeks. The 'schoolboy error' of failing to organise filming

with a clapperboard, plus contradictory input from John and Paul, compli-
cated Benson's task.

Like the film's style and content, the accompanying musical format
offered 'emergent' and 'residual' features. Unwilling to pad out the six-song
soundtrack with unrelated recordings, an innovative double EP with gate-
fold sleeve was released (in the UK). Its accompanying 24-page booklet
included a 'psychedelic-style' cartoon strip summary by Bob Gibson, but
also sported advertisements for the Beatles official fan club and its *Beatles
Monthly Book*, a publication running since 1963 (with Gibson a regular
contributor). As well as such publicity offering 'reassurance' to their long-
standing fan base (Neaverson 1997: 53), the move towards countercultural
impulses did not preclude the Beatles 'brand' from yet again being compre-
hensively commercialised.

Magical Mystery Tour, loosely centred on Ringo's ongoing arguments
with his widowed Aunt Jessica (Jessie Robins), follows a motley collec-
tion of characters on a coach trip across the English countryside, destination unknown. Interspersed with musical interludes, 'strange things begin
to happen' en route, seemingly orchestrated by a band of celestial magicians
(Beatles and Mal Evans), whose brief appearances are most noticeable for
John reprising (and arguably overegging) his camp stylings from *A Hard
Day's Night*. The tourists stop at an Army recruitment office, a racetrack,
restaurant and strip-club before concluding with the tuxedoed Beatles leading a Busby Berkeley-style dance number. The film premiered on British
television between broadcasts of a *This is Petula Clark* variety special and
Norman Wisdom's war comedy *The Square Peg* (Carstairs, 1959) at 8.35pm
on BBC1 on 26 December 1967 and, seen by up to 20 million viewers,
occasioned the first (and only) major critical panning of the Beatles' career.

James Green summarised the UK furore: 'It's a long day's night since
any TV show took the hammering that this Beatles fantasy received by tel-
ephone and in print. Take your pick from the words, "Rubbish, piffle, chaotic, flop, tasteless, nonsense, emptiness and appalling!" I watched it. There
was precious little magic, and the only mystery was how the BBC came to
buy it' (1967). Similar viewer responses – 'rubbish', 'nonsense' and 'they
needn't have bothered' – featured on the front page of the *Daily Mirror*
(Jenour 1967: 1), while the paper's television critic Mary Malone decried
how there was 'No magic in this Sad Beatles' Tour', only a 'chaotic' mess
with 'no aim' (1967). Henry Raynor's response indicated how the cross-
generational accord established by *A Hard Day's Night* had evaporated:

> Probably this was an attempt at a fantasy of wish-fulfilment, deco-
> rated with youthfully fashionable ideas, 'psychedelic' designs and the
> coarsely grainy photography which not very long ago was a sign of

spontaneity and originality. This was a programme to experience rather than understand; I was unfortunate – I lacked the necessary key.

(1967)

Several (older) critics saw not experimentation, only arrogance. James Thomas, noting how 'the bigger they are, the harder they fall ... and what a fall it was!', complained that 'the confusion was horrific' and concluded that 'the whole boring saga confirmed a long-held suspicion of mine that the Beatles are four rather pleasant young men who have made so much money that they can apparently afford to be contemptuous of the public' (1967). Douglas Marlborough's *Daily Mail* piece more concisely objected that 'It's colossal, the conceit of the Beatles' (1967).

The extent of the criticism led to the unparalleled (and potentially mistaken) move of McCartney immediately seeking to effect damage limitation through media outlets. He found broad support on television: 'if you watch it a second time it does grow on you,' he noted in an appearance on the following night's broadly-welcoming *The Frost Report* (BBC1). There was less sympathy from press interviews: 'There was no plot, so it was pointless trying to find one. It is like an abstract painting', he vainly told Robin Turner in an article nonetheless headed 'Even Beethoven Wasn't Great All the Time' (1967). The youth-centred *NME* disagreed, Norrie Drummond insisting the film had 'great merit', sharing qualities with 'a beautiful painting or a good book, something which one can go back to again and again, discovering something new each time' (1968: 3).

That loyal support aside, the UK's only positive press review came from Keith Dewhurst, for whom 'the poetry beyond professionalism of the Beatles' bettered all other Christmas television fare. He admitted of their film that

> Some of it was too condensed and too private, but the whole was an inspired freewheeling achievement and ... a kind of fantasy morality play about the grossness, warmth and stupidity of the audience whose adoration has set the Beatles free amongst the dreamscapes whose poignancy their photography caught so well.

(1967)

If so, that audience depiction was clearly not appreciated, since the BBC's subsequent reaction index – a number derived from quizzing a cross-sample of television viewers – scored its lowest-ever rating: 23% (Harris 2012).

Why this near-total rejection? Contextual factors are important here, both with the medium issuing the work and the media evaluating it. Production delays until 8 December with the lavish EP design, and the BBC banning 'I Am the Walrus' for its use of the word 'knickers', meant that *Magical Mystery*

Tour did not enjoy the lengthy pre-release musical momentum/familiarisation enjoyed by its predecessors. Far more importantly, though, colour was crucial to the film's formal radicality, so its initial transmission in black and white stripped the work of its aesthetic core, with monochrome rendering several musical sequences virtually meaningless. (Here Paul was [initially] mistaken: a repeat transmission in colour on BBC2 on 5 January 1968 – when the UK had only 200,000 colour television sets (Merritt 1987: 7) – would not reverse the weight of public opinion). The film's content, though, could still hit home – in all senses of the term. With the Beatles still the nation's major cultural draw, their film's understandable primetime scheduling on a domestically placed medium allowed it to penetrate the country's most intimate spaces, catching spectators (and critics) unaware and potentially transforming the depoliticised and atomised environment of the television-adorned living-room into a site of subversion and mass cultural destabilisation. This unexpected discomfort was again not appreciated.

Secondly, one needs to qualify the widespread notion that suddenly, 'for the first time since they'd worn leather jackets at a Young Conservatives dance, the Beatles found themselves being collectively slagged off' (Norman 2003: 324–5). The admission by McCartney in June 1967 (in interviews for *Queen* in the UK and *Life* in the US) that the Beatles had taken LSD, an experimentation moreover endorsed by the erstwhile universally respected Epstein, occasioned debate in Parliament and an official condemnation from the Home Office which, just like later film reviewers, had declared itself 'horrified' at such a stance (Brown and Gaines 1984: 218–9). This was the UK's minor-key version of Lennon's 'bigger than Jesus' furore, and with the first work following their drug-taking admission seemingly rife with drug-influenced imagery and simulated 'trips', here was the chance for the newly antagonistic conservative press to retaliate. While happy to accept the group's (more abstract) musical experimentation, the critical majority were not yet ready to *see* their family favourites move from lovable young mop-tops over into the counterculture, certainly not in front of the children, and certainly not at light-entertainment-expectant Christmas time.

The poor UK critical reception afforded to *Magical Mystery Tour* discouraged American networks from acquiring the rights – at an estimated fee of $1 million (Harry 1984: 66), while its sub-hour length worked against a theatrical release. All was not doom and gloom, however. While only limited US screenings were held in Los Angeles and San Francisco in May 1968, later rentals to US universities and colleges brought in $2 million – dwarfing the initial £9,000 payment from the BBC (O'Dell 2002: 72). The expanded American soundtrack album, released in November and including recent hits such as 'Strawberry Fields Forever' and 'Penny Lane', grossed $8 million in its first ten days and topped the US charts for eight weeks.

Import copies even put the album at number 31 in the UK album chart, where the EP became the country's first ever million-seller (Coryton and Murrells 1990: 170). In all, advance record orders meant the film was, like *A Hard Day's Night*, well in profit before its screen premiere (O'Dell 2002: 72). Moreover, the work has subsequently undergone a positive (if not complete) reassessment, especially following a digitised DVD release in 2012. This has come both from filmmakers, notably Martin Scorsese's acknowledgement of its influence on his work (*Arena ... 2012*), and from film historians, David E. James affirming how it 'marked a real innovation for the possibilities of a genuinely populist, English, music-based psychedelic film' (2016: 163).

Cultural historians agree that 'The film's hostile reception in Great Britain didn't preclude the film from furthering the Beatles' counterculture credentials' (Frontani 2007: 162). Most, though, note a particular Beatles 'twist': Ian MacDonald sees an emphasis on 'sending up consumerism, showbiz, and the clichés of the media' in 'their version of the counter-culture's view of mainstream society' (1994: 204); for Bob Neaverson their presentation 'confirmed and crystallised the Beatles' recently acquired media image as the central figureheads of their own all-embracing, and therefore paradoxically populist, vision of counter-culture' (1997: 69). Just how populist this vision is remains debateable, though, from the on-screen evidence. After the confinements and chasings of their first two film ventures, prime motivations for the Beatles here are to escape their celebrity image – hence taking on the guise of fellow travellers on a mystery tour; and to leave behind their 'cartoon' depictions – even the ever-lovable Ringo is here argumentative and disrespectful to his older relative.

At the same time, the film works to reinforce the individuality lightly expounded in *A Hard Day's Night* but largely expunged in *Help!*. Whilst each member contributes discrete sequences to the pie-chart script and extemporised direction, they seldom interact as a group, bar varyingly parodic performances in the (culturally emergent) 'I Am the Walrus' and the (culturally residual) 'Your Mother Should Know'. Instead, they take on myriad fictional roles from travel agents to waiters. Add in the fact that, uniquely, the attendant record cover had their faces masked and it becomes a personally liberating but professionally alienating strategy. Problematising conventional modes of pop group celebrity representation, here instead are the 'real' Beatles, 'presenting an image more consistent with the Beatles' perception of themselves' (Frontani 2007: 16). Once more, this is both true and not true.

Duality is again key as the group's mystery trip, moving beyond a voguish UK version of Haight-Ashbury, is pointedly interlaced with personal cultural memories from their youth, memories more redolent of Richard

Hoggart (and raucous Hamburg). Contemporary drug-infused psychedelic enactments are certainly widely present – the title track's opening 'roll up' can be read as an invitation to prepare a joint, while Paul with his 'head in a cloud' in the last-filmed zoom-heavy sequence for 'The Fool on the Hill' offers a distinctly lysergic pastoralism. In between, alongside non-diegetic inserts of a waving, bouncing, cheering then swaying crowd, à la mode surrealist tropes are regularly deployed. This is, perhaps over-deliberately, recreated in the visual correlation to 'I Am The Walrus' where, with split-screen editing and solarised filming, the kaftan-clad Beatles sport animal masks alongside conjoined egg-headed followers and (prefiguring *Yellow Submarine*) against a swaying quartet of music-tamed policemen. It plays more validly in the restaurant scene where, to the accompaniment of (the unreleased home-made track) 'Jessie's Dream', Pirandello the waiter (Lennon) continually shovels spaghetti onto Aunt Jessie's plate – the impromptu realisation of a dream experienced by John the night before (Pieper and Path 2005: 319).

However, other incidents recall deep-rooted Liverpudlian cultural practices rather than Surrealism's 'omnipotence of dreams.' In addition to the charabanc concept itself, with Ringo et al. lubricating a singalong of standards like 'When Irish Eyes are Smiling' with swigs from bottled beer, the tag wrestling and tug-of-war contest were familiar to the group from local halls and their teenage village fetes (*Arena* … 2012). The glitzy finale of 'Your Mother Should Know', complete with the 160-strong Peggy Spencer Dance Troupe, pays an overblown homage to the ballroom dancing predominantly popular with the Beatles' own working and lower-middle classes (Nott 2015: 39). To explore one example in detail. The strip-club scene (filmed at Paul Raymond's Soho Revuebar) was a staple of male coach outings cf. *Rattle of a Simple Man* (Box, 1964). Autobiographically, the scene referenced the Beatles' own performance origins, notably their pre-Hamburg July 1960 booking backing 'Janice the Stripper' at Allan Williams' New Cabaret Artistes club in Liverpool (Lewisohn 2013: 348–9). Intertextually, the backing track to Jan Carson's act has a title, 'Death Cab For Cutie', originating in Hoggart's study of working-class culture as an 'imitation' of popular pseudo-American post-war pulp fiction (1957: 212). The casting of performers such as professional accordionist Shirley Evans and music-hall veteran Nat Jackley as 'Rubber Man' Happy Nat similarly gesture towards the northern popular culture of the Beatles' youth from and against which they forged their 'youth culture' personae. With continuing Beatle film duplicity, those formative practices are simultaneously satirised yet celebrated.

Furthermore, while the film largely prizes experimentation over narrative comprehension, its satirical intent is plentiful. With firm countercultural intent, as Michael Frontani notes, it persistently 'displays an assault on the mores of straight society' (2007: 166). The tour's first stop is at a military recruitment office, complete with Kitchener's 'I Want You' poster and over-sized jingoistic Union Jack. Here the trippers dutifully line up as the Army Sergeant (Beatles regular Victor Spinetti) bellows incomprehensible instructions at them – until temporarily stymied by Ringo's gentle interrogative 'why?'. The sequence not only carries over themes and iconography from *Help!* but more pointedly and personally functions as a parodic re-enactment of (the narrowly avoided) military service. The officer's sole intelligible order to 'Get your bloody hair cut!' offers a more explicit conscription-centred confrontation than that enacted with the train commuter in *A Hard Day's Night*, and those regular early interviews with journalists. Alongside the decaying authority of the armed forces, the Church is similarly mocked after the marathon run when a group of highly competitive and sore-losing vicars make unpleasant gestures at the race winners. So too are the police. Uniting church and state and underlining the film's youthful surrealism, Neaverson compares the incongruous and infantilised quartet of police officers dancing atop a blast wall during 'I Am the Walrus' – Lennon's 'pretty little policemen in a row' – to the piano-chained priests pulled along in *Un Chien Andalou/An Andalusian Dog* (Buñuel, 1929) (1997: 63). Even the strip-club scene, where an animated 'CENSORED' sign covering Jan Carson's bared breasts keeps all 'within the bounds of British decency', lampoons the mid-1960s Clean Up TV brigade of Mary Whitehouse and the wary BBC itself. Here (broadcast indecently early in the BBC schedule) was a further iteration of the decade's vogue for debunking, progressing from *That Was the Week That Was* into (the McCartney-welcoming) *The Frost Report*.[5]

These, though, were all black-and-white creations, and colour is key to *Magical Mystery Tour*, from the Plaxton-bodied Bedford VAL14 coach with its yellow livery and rainbow-lettered eponymous logo, through to the multi-coloured fashions ranging from the magicians' red costumes to Paul's stripy Fair Isle tank-top – their subdued Dougie Millings suits now a distant (yet only two-year-old) memory. Allied to the use of colour is the film's countercultural creativity – probably chemically enhanced, but definitely extolling contemplation. During his raga-related 'Blue Jay Way' number George, in an orange suit and lotus position, plays an imaginary (chalk-drawn) keyboard. However, in contrast to the mechanical and regimented pop art reproductions of his image in *A Hard Day's Night*, here there is a proliferation of kaleidoscopic and prismatic imagery, double-exposures and superimpositions more akin to the closing credits of *Help!*. Effected by Ringo, credited as the film's Director of Photography, they create a more organic, richly colour-laden and narrative-free avant-garde 'film within a film', projected to the coach party in a meta-context equally reminiscent of *Help!*'s opening (see Figure 3.1).

Much like John Lennon later describing his first experience of acid as 'real life in Cinemascope' (Norman 2008: 426), this sequence can readily be interpreted as visual 'tripping', with George 'a Leary-inspired advocate of mind-expanding drugs' (Neaverson 1997: 69). Similarly, his (29 times) repeated 'don't be long' lyric is alternatively readable as 'don't belong' – a call for the young to 'turn on, tune in, drop out' from Western society (Inglis 2010: 10). However, what Harrison witnessed during his August 1967 sojourn in California, beginning at Blue Jay Way in the Hollywood Hills and moving on to Haight-Ashbury, had occasioned a complete disillusionment with the effects of LSD on US youth culture (Beatles 2000: 259). In the song's later visual correlation, the overlaying of George with domestic and Hindu sacred animals, plus the number's pace-contrasting placement immediately after the frantic car-chase marathon, mark it more fully as an index of Harrison's increased interest in Eastern mysticism and its meditative practices (initiated while making *Help!*). Here, as Jonathan Gould more cogently interprets, is George 'yogically floating on air' (2007: 456).

This vision is expanded in the polychromatic highlight of *Magical Mystery Tour*, appearing en route with the imagery accompanying the group-composed

Figure 3.1. Magical Mystery Tour – George does Raga, Ringo does Dada.

instrumental 'Flying'. Addressing his (coach and television) audience, cou-
rier 'Jolly' Jimmy Johnson (Derek Royle) contrasts the journey's 'not very
inspiring' left-side view of the countryside with the right-hand vista, where-
upon an eyeline match reveals a correlative flight across a lunar-like landscape – in fact aerial outtakes of Iceland purloined from *Dr. Strangelove*
(Kubrick, 1964) – where the footage is tinted with deeply saturated colours,
a fab four of green, blue, yellow and red. Redolent of Warhol's pop art silk-
screens, the daring and disorientating colour-palette of Antonioni's *Il Deserto
Rosso/Red Desert* (1964) and the recording studio sessions in *Help!*, here the
audio-visual disruption of place, time and mood provides what many again
adjudge the film's most concentrated expression of LSD-fuelled liberation,
a sequence that, rising to 'colour-filtered cloud imagery, closely resembles a
simulated "trip"' (Neaverson 1997: 65). Once more, though, with Johnson's
co-courier Wendy Winters (Miranda Forbes) offering potential orientation
by wearing a sparkling pink bindi, the imagery equally offers another 'third
eye' realisation of the counterculture's growing penchant for transcendental
meditation. It was headline news when, on 25 August, the Beatles boarded
at Euston Station the 'Mystical Special' to study with the Maharishi Mahesh
Yogi in Bangor, North Wales – their location when Brian Epstein died. Their
subsequent film's 'Flying' sequence offers an earnest vision of the Beatles in
the Bardo, above and beyond mere earthly chaos – and criticism.

Which was just as well, given the opprobrium heaped on *Magical
Mystery Tour* – and the BBC: 'Whoever authorised the showing of the
film on BBC1 should be condemned to a year squatting at the feet of the
Maharishi Mahesh Yogi' opined the *Daily Sketch* (27 December 1967). It
was thrown into greater relief by the uniform praise that had been accorded
to the Beatles' summer album *Sgt. Pepper's Lonely Hearts Club Band*.
The group's popular recuperation would come from a film inspired by that
album. The reference here is not to the film *called Sgt. Pepper's Lonely
Hearts Club Band* (Schultz, 1978), produced by Brian Epstein's erstwhile business partner Robert Stigwood and featuring the Bee Gees as the
eponymous Band. This would receive a fiercer panning than even *Magical
Mystery Tour*, David Ansen relatively restrained in labelling it 'a film with
a dangerous resemblance to wallpaper' (1978: 42). Instead, the Beatles'
recovery would necessitate a reversal of their move towards agency and
autonomy, being a project they had not authored and (initially) barely tolerated – United Artists' animated cartoon film *Yellow Submarine*.

Yellow Submarine – production and reception

The film's genesis can be traced back to November 1964, when Brian Epstein
sold the group's animated rights to Al Brodax's US-based King Features

company, authorising fifty-two half-hour shows and the use of two Beatles songs in each. *The Beatles* premiered on ABC television in September 1965, immediately broke all American television ratings, and lasted as long as the group itself, only ending in September 1969 (Reiter 2008: 83–6). Far from being flattered by the project, however, it proved a constant irritant for the group who received little financial return and zero creative input – or character development as mop-topped caricatures anachronistically delivered the psychedelic sounds of 'Strawberry Fields Forever' and 'All You Need Is Love'. Nonetheless, with McCartney flattered by Brodax's promise of a feature-length animation based on his 'Yellow Submarine' composition, and the group sensing an easy absentee conclusion to their three-picture deal with United Artists (even their voices would be given to actors), contracts were signed.

However, misgivings intensified when the film's realisation was entrusted to George Dunning and John Coates, whose Soho-centred TV Cartoons company had churned out numerous episodes for the abhorred television series. Dunning, though, was determined to use the opportunity afforded by a year-long schedule and $1 million/£350,000 budget (Neaverson 1997: 82) to make a more elaborate, artistically achieved film and he commissioned international input from several experimental animators. Though Heinz Edelmann, the Czech-born artistic designer on West Germany's innovative *Twen* magazine, was brought in to manage the overall visual style and develop the central characters, the problems encountered in securing a coherent screenplay are evident in writing credits listing Brodax, Lee Minoff, Jack Mendelsohn and future *Love Story* author Erich Segal (plus, uncredited, Mersey poet Roger McGough).

The root causes of the various inspirations, impediments (and industrial disputes) are fiercely contested by those involved (Hieronimus 2002: 216–32), but consensus reigns that the project was close to stalling until George Martin presented pre-release tapes of *Sgt. Pepper's Lonely Hearts Club Band*. This proved a revitalizing source of creativity, notably triggering the colour-filled Pepperland, and its nemesis, the hateful Blue Meanies (Harry 1984: 37). The Beatles' new album also informed the movie's soundscape, with five songs enlisted (and 'Fixing A Hole', later dropped, inspiring the Sea of Holes episode). These numbers did not re-appear on the *Yellow Submarine* soundtrack album which, uniquely not the main motivation for a theatrically-released Beatles movie, was rather thrown together. The Beatles fulfilled their original song quota through cast-offs from other projects, with side two filled by George Martin's Stravinsky-inflected orchestral score.

Undermining any cross-media synergistic potential, the album's release was delayed until January 1969, largely to avoid interference with the November release of *The Beatles* aka *White Album*, and would provide a (relatively) indifferent financial return, failing to top the album charts in either the US or UK. Nonetheless, when the Beatles saw how their music was being visually interpreted they adjudged it a worthy adjunct to their new mature intellectual status. Hence, they agreed to a brief live action coda appearance where they invited an international audience to join them in musical unison, finally making the *Yellow Submarine* project 'all together now'. Borne aloft on a flood of marketing and merchandising – including die cast models, jigsaws and 'the world's first ever full-colour paperback' (Buskin 1994: 84) – the last-minute-group-endorsed movie received a star-studded premiere on Wednesday 17 July 1968 at the London Pavilion on Piccadilly Circus. The American premiere, shorn of the 'Hey Bulldog' section to keep the film under 90 minutes, followed on 13 November.

The film tells of how Pepperland is overrun by Blue Meanies, who imprison its protectors, Sgt. Pepper's Lonely Hearts Club Band, petrify the inhabitants and rid the land of colour and music. Old Fred escapes in his yellow submarine to Liverpool, where he recruits the Beatles to help his rescue mission. On the return journey they cross various seas, experience adventures and pick up the loquacious Jeremy Hillary Boob, PhD. In Pepperland the band find instruments, liberate Sgt. Pepper's Band and orchestrate the Blue Meanies' defeat with the restorative power of love and music.

Especially after the critical mauling handed out seven months previously to the 'amateurish' *Magical Mystery Tour*, the animated *Yellow Submarine* was a distinct critical success, at home and abroad. 'It is a fantastic achievement, not only a new kind of entertainment, but a new step forward in animation techniques,' enthused Nina Hibbin (1968). Dilys Powell concurred, writing that 'in speed of movement and density of reference it sets a new standard for the narrative cartoon' (1968). Alongside the artistic invention, most critics seemed particularly pleased to rediscover the 'safe' and lovable Fab Four from earlier media incarnations. Patrick Gibbs noted, almost with relief, that 'the Beatles spirit is here if not the flesh – their good-natured gusto, their kindly curiosity, their sympathy with their fellow men and their lack of pretentiousness are all summed up here with gaiety' (1968), while Dick Richards spelled out how 'it is the personality and pull of the Beatles themselves which makes this a worthwhile ninety minutes and makes us forgive the bleak memory of the group's *Magical Mystery Tour*' (1968). Exonerating the freshly-repackaged Beatles, the few critical caveats suggested the film was too long – for David Nathan 'about three-quarters of the way through, the sub sinks' (1968) – and, if anything, too inventive for its own good, Margaret Hinxman concluding that 'there's so much variety, it's just too overpowering for complete pleasure' (1968).

Antiphonal voices were singular. America's *Time* magazine was most negative: noting that 'the score includes several hits by the Beatles and just as many misses', it pursued this 'curious case of artistic schizophrenia' by warning that 'the plot and the animation seem too square for hippies and too hip for squares. Children, as usual, are caught between' ('Bad Trip' 1968). In the UK Felix Barker, so taken with the group's Lester films, now predicted that most people would 'hate every five thousand two hundred and twenty seconds of this cartoon' – if they could get in, Barker further cautioning the general public that 'you won't be able to get near the box office for hippies, flower people, Beatle-crushers, love-inners and sit-downers' (1968).

Lack of access would prove a premonitory pronouncement, but for reasons of exhibition rather than exhibitionists. In America the film performed decently, and a global gross box office has been cited at $8 million (Hieronimus 2002: 303). However, just three weeks after its London premiere, articles ran in most British daily newspapers that Rank was considering dropping the film due to disappointing attendances at its dozen UK pre-release theatres (Glynn 2008: 151). This purely financial explanation did not hold water, though, and was fiercely contested by United Artists and Apple, with published box-office receipts for the London Pavilion – a capacity £7000 per week – putting the weight of evidence in their favour (Harry 1992: 712). So why the curtailed distribution and exhibition? Had Rank erred on its financial calculations, or did they sense a more subversive agenda, something more countercultural than a simple kiddies' cartoon? What had the critics praised that Rank baulked at?

The answer can, perhaps, be found in the enthusiastic review of Alexander Walker, not alone in claiming that the film had captured the cultural *zeitgeist*:

> *Yellow Submarine* is the key film of the Beatles era. It's a trip through the contemporary mythology that the quartet from Merseyside have helped create... a pop voyage that sails under the psychedelic colours of Carnaby Street to the turned-on music of "Sgt. Pepper's Lonely Hearts Club Band". It combines sensory stimulation with the art of the now in a way that will appeal to teenage ravers and Tate Gallery goers alike.
>
> (1968)

If, as will be shown, this is a problematic assessment, it still sets up viable parameters for investigation. Let us start with the appeal to those (loosely-aged) 'teenage ravers'.

Animated counterculture's acceptance

Yellow Submarine opens with a voiceover – 'Once upon a time, or maybe twice, there was an unearthly paradise called Pepperland. Eighteen thousand leagues beneath the sea it lay. Or lie, I'm not too sure' – that immediately sets up an interpretive uncertainty, an undermining doubt that will continue to the film's conclusion. It is followed, though, by a visual exposition of reassuring narrative binarity. A string quartet practise in the park, while around them people picnic, children dance, and their mother receives a bouquet of roses. Fade to an overlooking mountain ridge, where stand fierce, regimented figures ready to attack, their leader goose-stepping and barking orders. With its generic conclusion inscribed in this exposition, *Yellow Submarine* functions fully as a child-friendly fantasy on the forces of good overcoming those of evil, a return to the family-focused fun eschewed in the audience-alienating *Magical Mystery Tour*.

Nonetheless, since the production team were determined to create 'a genuine celebration of the "60s youth rebellion"' (Hieronimus 2002: 94–5), the film can equally be read as an allegorical play on contemporary states of consciousness and governance, the Beatles enacting 'a kind of hippie parable about the power of love' (Frontani 2007: 174). Stylistically, that opening scene places an adult knowingness alongside simple, child-like forms. A similar cross-generational resonance of meaning resides in the extant title, for while the group always claimed that 'Yellow Submarine' was a children's song, a 'yellow submarine' was also the code-name for the popular yellow, elongated narcotic pill Nembutal. The narrative's sea journey, prompted by the song, is easily interpretable as another Beatles-led simulated 'trip', a fuller recreation of the drug-inspired visions than had been possible with the use of real people and locations in their recent charabanc catastrophe.

The epicentre of this psychedelic re-run is seen to lie, or lay, like *Help!* in 'Swinging London'. As the submarine leaves Liverpool Pier for Pepperland, we hear the rising orchestral glissandi from 'A Day in the Life', generally interpreted, following on from the vocal line 'I'd love to turn you on', as an electronic trip. A rapid montage of postcards and photographs gravitates (as did the Beatles) from Merseyside to the Metropolis, while the plunge into the Thames initiates a consciousness-expanding journey leading to karmic union. The ensuing soundtrack, borrowing heavily from *Sgt. Pepper's Lonely Hearts Club Band*, amplifies such readings. Ian MacDonald labels the *Sgt. Pepper* sound, especially its use of echo and reverb, as 'the most authentic aural simulation of the psychedelic experience ever created' (1994: 220), and the songs employed in *Yellow Submarine* display copious amounts of drug-inspired imagery. Exhibit A, 'Lucy in the Sky with Diamonds', despite Lennon's explanation of innocent filial origins, can extrapolate from the title's initialism to be read as an hallucinatory LSD trip. The 'throwaway' songs given to the film are equally open to alternative interpretations. 'All Together Now', following the infantile 'Black, White, Green, Red' by asking 'Can I take my friend to bed?', subverts childish innocence with references to the sexual revolution widely advertised yet for most – *pace* Peter Whitehead's quasi-documentary *Tonite Let's All Make Love in London* (1967) – so difficult to experience in the so-called Summer of Love.

Out with its visual and sonic 'tripping', the film is open to a wealth of allegorical readings. The Blue Meanies and associates in particular lend themselves to symbolic treatment, at industrial, social and political levels. Dunning rigorously eschewed the Disney Corporation's animation style with his stuttering cartoon movements and its working practices with his outsourced technical staff. His Meanies bear unmistakable Mickey Mouse ears, redolent of the nemesis organisation's aggressive monopoly of animated film. Dunning's design was prescient as, capitalising on the interest raised by this production, Disney re-released its own animated musical, *Fantasia* (1940), which, with full exhibition guaranteed, in Britain far outsold *Yellow Submarine*. (To which one can add *Peter Pan* (1953), filling the Rank void when the Beatles film was suddenly withdrawn).

These Meanie meanings can continue. David Bowman conjectures whether the Kinky Boot Beasts are reminders of the aggressive girl fans in their King's Road gear who would assault the Beatles and their wives (1972: 178), while Dilys Powell suggests that the Ferocious Flying Glove, pointing its finger as a prelude to destruction, offers 'a dig at the censor' (1968). These characters, alongside Jack the Nipper, the Butterfly Stomper et al. with their paranoid fear of music, can also be interpreted as the myriad troubled bodies that 'came together' as the record-burning hordes from the group's final 1966 American tour – or even the unsympathetic critics from all sections of the media that blackened the Beatles' image by so vilifying *Magical Mystery Tour*.

Above all, though, these unfeeling adversaries invite interpretation as wider symbols of state oppression. In appearance and *modus operandi* they resemble the British police, wearing blue uniforms, using fierce dogs and carrying weapons to hit people on the head. American critics noted how the Chief Meanie wears cowboy boots, spurs and a robber mask, suggestive of American cultural imperialism. Foreign populations are bled dry by the Big Apple, and the Pepperlanders' period costumes act as reminders of 'the good old days before the Americanisation of England' i.e. before the arrival of youth culture (Bowman 1972: 178).

Most evidently, though, one can read the Blue Meanies as general forces of European fascism. Old newsreel footage of Adolf Hitler served

Edelmann as a model for the Chief Blue Meanie's movements, and such source contexts are narratively foregrounded as the Meanies enact military subjugation with missiles landing on the idyllic, pastoral bandstand and sending the audience fleeing in panic. When hit by bolts of lightning the citizens are petrified and drained of colour, only for Apple Stompers to continue crushing their motionless victims. As the Pepperland pogrom intensifies, a tear falls down the lens of a man's glasses: when a girl's spinning windmill is bitten off by a Snapping Turk another tear falls. Meanwhile the glove rounds up and tries to crush potential escapees by bashing its fist on the ground. George Orwell's dystopian vision in *1984*, which also ends with two trickling tears, was to picture the future as 'a boot stamping on a human face – forever' (1998 [1948]: 230). That future here takes the form of a giant blue-gloved fist pounding on the innocent – repeatedly.

Nonetheless, on witnessing such tyranny, John, by then the most explicit socio-political conscience of the Beatles, makes no reference to police or military brutality, to Fascist ghettoization or even concurrent Vietnam bombings. Instead, combining childhood recollection and the forces of reaction, he remarks how the chief Blue Meanie reminds him of a more personal figure of authority, 'my old English teacher'. It is a comment that returns us to the origins of Western youth culture and its musical engine in the school-set *Blackboard Jungle*, a reminder amidst adult messages in a child-like idiom of the perennial teenage need to rebel against the nearest embodiment of establishment authority: their schoolteacher. It is, also, psychologically, a credible pronouncement, with Lennon's hatred of his Quarry Bank schooling, especially its English lessons, the root of a lifelong vituperation at having been so 'looked down on' when young (Wenner 1973: 163–4).

John's more sedate pronouncement here, though, primarily functions as a 'typical' facetious remark from the Beatles in a film replete with shamelessly poor punning and adenoidal deadpan ruminations. This is perhaps most successfully employed when Ringo, questioning his senses as the submarine stalks him across Liverpool, encapsulates the film's intentions by telling himself 'It must be a pigment of my imagination'. As in the television cartoon, however, sound and vision clash. The look of 'the newly furry Fabs' (Ingham 2006: 165) is drawn (bar Paul's moustache) from their appearance in Swedish director Peter Goldmann's promotional videos for 'Strawberry Fields Forever' and 'Penny Lane' (February 1967) (see Figure 3.2). However, the unending wordplay, tapping into the northern music-hall roots of the Beatles' repartee, anachronistically retains the 'ad-libbed' humour so central to the group's early popularity, in person as in film – only here with a few current, hip sayings tacked on.

Figure 3.2. Yellow Submarine – counterculture from the Furry Fab Four.

In its general depiction of the separate Beatle characters, *Yellow Submarine* similarly mines their Richard Lester movies. Once more the narrative centres largely on Ringo who, as in *A Hard Day's Night*, walks alone and lonely through city backstreets, and who, as in *Help!*, serves as catalyst for the plot, initiating the group's involvement in Pepperland. John is the intellectual of the group, the 'clever lad' able to speak visible words and, in the Sea of Holes, conjecture on their involvement 'in Einstein's space-time continuum theory, relatively speaking that is'. Paul, first seen after conducting a classical concert on the Pier and able to identify the Father Times because 'I read it in a book', is again presented as the most openly 'cultured' of the quartet, the Beatle most at ease with the back-catalogue. Only George is seen entirely through his new media image as an exponent of the Eastern arts of transcendental meditation: floating to the ground from atop Sgt. Pepper's statue at the film's conclusion, he provides the calming animus amidst the frantic animation.

In purely narrative terms, it is John with his Frankenstein transformations – 'I've just had the strangest dream!' – and George with his gentle 'all in the mind' levitations that most overtly evoke a countercultural/drug-fuelled consciousness. Equally, it is their compositions that, freed of narrative progression, receive an animated interpretation most correlative with the hallucinogenic experience. Nonetheless, all of *Yellow Submarine*'s musical sequences serve to summarise, condense and foreground the youth-centred art styles present throughout the Beatles films, and elaborate what Alexander Walker termed the cartoon's appeal to 'Tate Gallery goers'.

Yellow Submarine presents styles and imagery taken from a range of contemporary paintings, prints and designs. Contemporary reviews, seeking to convey the eclecticism on show cited *inter alia* pop artists Claes Oldenburg and Robert Rauschenberg, Saul Steinberg and Graham Sutherland, newspaper colour supplements and Dr. Seuss, Salvador Dalí and even Hieronymus Bosch (Glynn 2008: 148). Special mention is merited for Aubrey Beardsley, a leading figure in *fin de siècle* aestheticism, whose work, re-evaluated in a hugely successful 1966 exhibition at London's Victoria and Albert Museum, realigned him as an artist challenging normative gender and sexual categories, and precipitated his elevation to the position of the counterculture's style guru. Most evident in the animation sequences designed by Charles Jenkins, the style of the art editor for *The Yellow Book* – a periodical resembling the underground's *Oz* magazine in its notoriety and short life[6] – pervades the *Yellow Submarine* film. This was instantly noted by John Coleman who, resisting the majority's affectionate reading of Jeremy, was instead reminded 'eerily of that diseased dwarf who appears in a bottom corner of some Beardsley' (1968). Such influences occasioned a full review for *Yellow Submarine* in the Art section of Britain's *Observer* newspaper where Nigel Gosling averred that the film 'packs in more stimulation, sly art-references and pure joy into ninety minutes than a mile of exhibitions of op and pop and all the mod cons' (1968). Let us take Gosling's exhibitions in turn.

The op is foregrounded in the arresting black-and-white imagery of the 'Sea of Holes' sequence, borrowing blatantly – as did the youth-oriented fashion industry – from the mid-1960s work of Bridget Riley. In dot pictures such as *Fission* (1963), *Pause* and *Where* (both 1964), Riley's elimination of colour and repetition of single geometrical shapes simultaneously established a stable pattern and induced an optical illusion, creating 'metaphors of unease, closely tuned uncertainties of reading' (Hughes 1991: 389). *Yellow Submarine* replicates this process of perception, pausing on the individual black dots when the Beatles are first sneezed into the sea before sweeping over, under, through and across its myriad holes (see Figure 3.3). This progression both creates a scale for the sea's sheer size and induces what Andrew Graham-Dixon calls the 'subversive, narcotic disorientation of the senses upon the viewer' (1996: 227).

Pop art influences pervade the film, especially those of (the ubiquitous) Andy Warhol, with, for Bob Neaverson, 'the most obvious homage to his style' residing in the 'Eleanor Rigby' sequence which 'bears striking

Figure 3.3. Yellow Submarine – living the life of Riley.

iconographical and textural resemblance to his mid to late sixties polymer paint and silk screen prints' (1997: 86). The sequence, though, is more multimedia and less celebrity-obsessed than Warhol's habitual work and merits explication. To explore one segment in detail. Immediately after the title credits blackout, George Martin's orchestral score seems briefly to match an idyllic mood of sunrise behind the distant Liver Building, until ceding via mid-distance terraced houses to a front row of eight blaring chimneys, calling the city's inhabitants to labour. As Paul sings twice of looking at 'all the lonely people', we see, through a street-door's transom-glass, a narrow strip of live action black-and-white footage showing dark figures trudging to work, stepping in time to the music, talking to no-one. The absence of colour links back to the repressed Pepperland, much as the soullessness resonates with the source of George Martin's string accompaniment, Bernard Herrmann's score for the dystopic *Fahrenheit 451* (Truffaut, 1966). A later use of live filming equates this passage to the rural labour shown on the Indian sub-continent, a visual reminder that the 1960s did not swing for everyone. Beneath the alienated workforce, an indifferent white bulldog, draped in the Union Jack, intimates how Britain's national success depends upon mass exploitation, both at home and abroad. The final chorus envelops the middle class, showing a series of white collar workers, identical and anonymous in their bowler hats, black coats and umbrellas – Warhol mixing with Magritte. The sequence is not without hope, however: Stephanie Fremaux cogently views the images of a motorcyclist with his psychedelic-patterned helmet and a contemplative angel on the rooftop as reflecting 'the promise the youth culture, the young creatives and thinkers, can bring to the drudgery of conformity and traditional values' (2018: 109).

Gosling's 'all the mod cons' move us beyond the already culturally 'respectable' fields of op or pop art and *Yellow Submarine* in its most daring sequences looks instead to graphic artists that were themselves a part of the drug-taking, countercultural underground. The flashing, multicoloured portraits of the Beatles that conclude 'Only A Northern Song' are informed, more than Warhol, by the four psychedelic posters by US photographer Richard Avedon, first published in January 1968. Beginning on America's West Coast, this poster style crossed to the British underground, notably influencing 'Hapshash and the Coloured Coat', the *nom de plume* of the graphic artists/avant-garde musicians Nigel Weymouth and Michael English, a duo seeking that their work should 'circumnavigate the rational' and 'become part of the trip' (Lowey and Prince 2014: 56–63). Hapshash notably promoted the activities of London's UFO (Unlimited Freak Out) Club, a focal point – alongside the Roundhouse – for Britain's counterculture. As described by George Melly, this was 'the first spontaneous and successful attempt to produce a total environment involving music, light and people' seeking 'mind expansion and hallucination at the service of the destruction of the non-hip and the substitution of "love", in the special, rather nebulous meaning that the word holds for the Underground' (1972: 136).

Yellow Submarine's fullest approximation to a UFO-style 'freak-out' comes in the concluding sequence accompanying 'It's All Too Much'. Described by Tim Riley as one of George's 'psychedelic outbursts' (1988: 243), Ian MacDonald sees the song lyrically as 'a *locus classicus* of English psychedelia' with time and place cohering in the line 'Show me that I'm everywhere and get me home for tea'. Here was the UK's version of the counterculture, alternative, but never fully oppositional. 'The revolutionary spirit then abroad in America and Europe was never reciprocated in comfortable (and sceptical) Albion, where tradition, nature and the child's-eye-view were the things which sprang most readily to the LSD-heightened Anglo-Saxon mind', Macdonald notes (1994: 228–9).

All of these 'Anglo-Saxon' aspects are given visual form in the animated amalgam that constitutes the film's grand finale. The sequence reverses the opening's monochrome destruction with a literal flowering of colour and giant golden letters – a Hapshash-style audio-visual 'happening'. Hidden Persuaders who earlier carried guns in their shoes now clink together mugs (of tea?), while a giant clown, transformed from a coulrophobic weapon into a child's innocent toy, grows a familiar patterning of foliage and rainbows. The cartoon Beatles appear in a summative collage featuring doves, letters, and flowers from Pepperland, all alongside strongmen, spectacles and superheroes from the Pier (before fading to the real-life Beatles dancing to the song's dying chords). In all, the sequence provides the visual correlative to an on-trend anthem, its intricate mix of colour and design integrating visions from Britain's counterculture and its eclectic artistic heritage (see Figure 3.4).

'Lucy in the Sky with Diamonds', the number potentially best lending itself to drug-fuelled expression, takes a different tack. Neaverson sees the sequence as 'a kind of animated Kandinsky on acid' (1997: 86–7), but rather than radical art, or acid, the animation here matches the retrospective mood of *Magical Mystery Tour* by feeding on more traditional modes of popular culture, rendering the number an internal and intertextual fantasy. The practices of the circus hall are referenced in prancing horses, a trapeze artist and saltimbanchi, while Hollywood film musicals are refigured both through a zoetroped, multicoloured Ginger Rogers and images of multiple dancing women where overhead angles recreate a Busby Berkeley-style geometric choreography. Rick Altman sees Berkeley's films as 'constituting the *locus classicus* of the musical's tendency to subordinate image to sound', the horizontal perspective subsuming individual referents such as hands, feet and costumed bodies into a single pattern. Here too the group aesthetic dominates – another case of 'all together now'. Considering the kaleidoscopic effect in a Berkeley work such as *Gold Diggers of 1933*, Altman finds that 'it is as if the screen were transformed into an electronically generated visual accompaniment to the music' (1987: 71). In

Figure 3.4. Yellow Submarine – a UFO sighting.

Dunning's animation, there is no 'as if' since the electronic transformation is visually achieved, 'made real'.

Later in the sequence, John also transforms – into 'illustrated song' performer Eddie Cantor, rotoscope dancing with Ruby Keeler. Here the classic 'cool' movements of the Hollywood heyday musical are overlaid with the impulsive brush strokes, rough edges and flashing colour changes of late-1960s design. It demonstrates the advantage of animation over mimesis. Unlike Berkeley's sequential causality – or the discrete set-piece essayed with 'Your Mother Should Know' in *Magical Mystery Tour* – both the visual order and randomness that replicates generic certainty and plot variation can now be presented simultaneously in an aesthetically achieved and thought-provoking cinematic doubleness.

Merging a Hollywood genre's back catalogue with a hallucinogenic Beatle, 'Lucy in the Sky with Diamonds' encapsulates the whole film's obsession with icons both past and present, illustrating how youth culture here moves forward by reaching back. Ringo's early Pier search with Old Fred turns up giant cut-outs of historical figures (General Custer), classical screen stars (Fred Astaire and Marilyn Monroe), contemporary comic-book heroes (The Phantom) and popular television characters (John Steed from *The Avengers* (ITV 1961–69)). It is a collage presentation heavily indebted to arguably the most iconic example of 1960s pop graphics, the album cover for *Sgt. Pepper's Lonely Hearts Club Band* itself. Photographed by Michael Cooper on 30 March 1967 and created by pop artists Peter Blake and Jann Howarth assembling 57 life-size photographed cut-outs and 9 waxwork figures, including the 1964 Beatles of *A Hard Day's Night* and their 'real' 1967 selves, the cover, as well as offering 'a guidebook to the cultural topography of the decade' (Inglis 2008: 93), is omnipresent in *Yellow Submarine*.

It features at a narrative level when the Beatles use similar life-size cut-outs to creep up unseen to the music stand. It is evident at a musical level if one accepts Tim Riley's description of the fade-out to 'All You Need Is Love' as 'the aural equivalent' to Blake and Howarth's montage (1988: 234). Above all, the film deploys the cover art's stylistic outlooks and influences – Beardsley, for instance, can be found album cover top left. The LP sleeve collects items indicative of the Beatles' countercultural preoccupations, with an Indian goddess, a portable television and (allegedly) a row of cannabis plants: images and sounds of Eastern religion, mediation and hallucination similarly pervade *Yellow Submarine*.

In particular, though, the film shares the fascination shown on the album cover – and in most psychedelic art – with Britain's Edwardian era. From its opening scenes, the inhabitants of Pepperland, grandfathers on pennyfarthings, servants and maids, soldiers in colourful uniforms, are consistently Edwardian in appearance. This love for bygone days, alongside the latest drugs, shapes the mise-en-scène, the music and even the message of *Yellow Submarine*. Mike Evans notes that 'it was the nostalgic element, rather than the outright "psychedelic", which predominated on the Pepper sleeve' (1984: 68), and this sentiment – central to UK counterculture – similarly feeds into the animated film. David Robinson had immediately noted how '*Yellow Submarine* seems to express a sort of retreat into a nostalgia for forgotten innocence,' a time of 'still fresh memories when the Beatle generation were babies' (1968). Consistent with the practices enlisted in *Magical Mystery Tour*, this journey back in time complements the film's musical soundscape, since the whole 'happening' that constituted *Sgt. Pepper's Lonely Hearts Club Band* can be seen, as George Melly noted, as 'finally a celebration of the past with its certainties and simplicities' (1972: 114).

For all its sophisticated studio-led experimentation and mature modulations in key and tempo, much of the Beatles' music at the time remained rooted in simple historical pastiche. 'When I'm Sixty-Four' offers a vogueish pre-war meta-pop pastiche redolent of the Temperance Seven and the Bonzo Dog Doo-Dah Band (guest performers in *Magical Mystery Tour* of the teen-tragedy pastiche 'Death Cab For Cutie'). The title track is, for MacDonald, 'a shrewd fusion of Edwardian variety orchestra and contemporary "heavy rock"' (1994: 206). Even 'Lucy in the Sky with Diamonds' signifies primarily for Wilfred Mellers as 'a revocation of a dream-world of childhood' (1973: 89). Elsewhere, the era's nostalgic raiding of 1930s film symbols can be seen in the cartoon appearance, alongside Busby Berkeley routines, of Boris Karloff's Frankenstein, King Kong, even the charging US Cavalry and Indians. Set among long skirts and bandstands, the arch-Edwardian Sgt. Pepper is himself rooted in an earlier world of clear hierarchy and (ostensible) social harmony.

Nonetheless, this is also a projected world promoting the counterculture's desired elision of work and leisure: 'it was twenty years ago today / Sgt. Pepper taught the band to *play*'. Similarly, amidst the idyllic and elegiac fantasy, the denouement of *Yellow Submarine* is clearly open to a contemporary political – and firmly countercultural – reading. The Beatles help to establish a new world order in Pepperland, but achieve this, as Neaverson notes, 'more through the redemptive consciousness-raising powers of music and nature than by violent retribution' (1997: 90). They do so with 'instruments at the ready'. Their musical performance of 'Sgt. Pepper's Lonely Hearts Club Band' frees their doppelgänger band and reanimates the population, returning colour to their costumes and smiles to their faces: the song climaxes with the re-emergence, literally from the underground, of the Sgt. Pepper statue. John takes the sting from the Flying G-love by removing its initial letter, sings his anthemic 'All You Need Is Love' and creates a protective word-web in the style of Robert Indiana's contemporary

'Love' paintings and sculptures. When the liberating Beatles take on a four-headed pale-blue Bulldog, we witness the classic image of hippiedom, with John pulling a gun which sprouts a flower in its barrel. The scene resonates with 'the Mobe', the mobilisation of 21 October 1967 when over 100,000 demonstrators – 'many dressed like the legions of Sgt. Pepper's band', noted Norman Mailer (1969: 108) – marched on the Pentagon and several placed flowers into the barrels of guns being held up by soldiers of the 82nd Airborne Division, defending the Pentagon itself. The peacenik image of guns and roses has endured, though that night, less visibly, the Pentagon soldiers would charge the protestors with their guns, causing several serious injuries.

Such belligerent retribution is absent from cartoon Pepperland, however, where the comforting *coup de grâce* comes from Jeremy, who recites 'some reference material' that covers the Chief Meanie in floral attire – a literal/cinematic enactment of the revolutionary force of 'flower power'. Defeated and reformed, the Chief agrees to John's Timothy Leary-like request to 'join us, hook up and otherwise co-mingle'. In contrast to the divisive violence of the arms-bearing United States, this is a pronouncement very much in the British spirit of *Sgt. Pepper's Lonely Hearts Club Band* where, as US poet and counterculture figurehead Allen Ginsberg stated, the Beatles 'offered an inclusive vision which, among other things, worked to defuse the tensions of the generation gap' (MacDonald 1994: 207). As it did of gender. The softening of the hyper-aggressive Chief with pink blooms – a signal for Noel Brown of 'the effeminisation (or perhaps bohemianisation) of the establishment' (2017: 170) – also continues the challenge to traditional notions of (hyper)masculinity evident from *A Hard Day's Night*. Overall, the sequence may register as simplistic, even childlike (Brown discusses the film in a survey of *British Children's Cinema*), but it also strikes an optimistic and holistic stance, a victory not of force but of making the enemy change their mindset.

The stance is consistent with the Beatles' earlier, accommodating film portrayals. Here, their victory also completes the voyage of discovery initiated when John, Paul, George and Ringo dived into the Thames accompanied by that swelling scale from 'A Day in the Life': a glissandi that for MacDonald symbolises 'a spiritual ascent from fragmentation to wholeness, achieved in the resolving E major chord' (1994: 203). If, in essence, youth culture offered to a generation a meaning and justification outwards via social interaction, the counterculture sought a more internal (and maturing) path to enlightenment, and if an overarching narrative drives *Yellow Submarine* it can be found in this spiritual search for wholeness, the sense not of group solidarity as with the fanbase in *A Hard Day's Night* but of an individual and inward quest. The press release labelled *Yellow Submarine* a 'Modyssey', and several Homeric allusions can be located. When the Beatles arrive in Pepperland, John declares their adventures to be 'rather reminiscent of the late Mr Ulysses'; in the Sea of Monsters he (mistakenly) calls out a Cyclops. More implicitly, Jeremy's wisdom, rather like Tiresias' advice, is not always heeded; the 'Lucy in the Sky' sequence can be seen as a distracting Siren.

Such parallels are at best approximate. Instead, the notion of odyssey links the film more directly to its partner in transcendental trippiness, Stanley Kubrick's *2001: A Space Odyssey* (1968). Shown concurrently in cinemas, *Yellow Submarine*'s Riley-esque Sea of Holes sequence finds an equivalent in the stargate journey that initiates the progression of David Bowman (Keir Duella)'s 'Odysseus figure' from human to Space Child, a passage where 'op-art patterns pulsate' like 'the hallucinogenic light show induced by LSD' (Walker et al. 1999: 190). This equating of inner and outer space also bears comparison with Richard Fleischer's recent sci-fi submarine film *The Fantastic Voyage* (1966), where the corporeal recreations again 'drew from the psychedelic light shows gaining popularity within countercultural environments' (Mathijs and Sexton 2011: 210). Rewinding further, the surreal universe marrying animation, science fiction and a pervasive black humour reveals a debt to the work of Polish artist-animators Jan Lenica (*Labirynt/ Labyrinth*, 1963) and Walerian Borowczyk (*Les Astronautes/Astronauts*, 1959) – their collaborative *Byl Sobi Raz/Once Upon a Time* (1957) returns us, Sea of Time-style, to the film's opening voiceover.

The explicit artistic eclecticism at play in *Yellow Submarine* could be catalogued *ad infinitum*, but to locate the film in its social context a comparison with a parallel television series is, in my opinion, most enlightening. I have elsewhere examined in detail the similarities between the Beatles film and the ITC series they greatly admired, *The Prisoner* (1967–68), produced – and later written – by Patrick McGoohan (Glynn 2013: 139–41). Here it is germane to note their similar exhibition difficulties, with the television show curtailed and shunted out to 11.15pm largely because, as Daniel O'Brien notes, 'it's alleged that ITC were unhappy with the escalating budgets and the show's too controversial drug references' (2000: 98). Textually, both relate the same story. Central characters are followed home, then transported to surreal worlds steeped in Edwardiana – animated Pepperland and Portmeirion's The Village. Each belies its surface 'whimsy' with a fearsome flying 'guard dog' – the stomping blue Glove and bouncing ball Rover. Each concludes with a lengthy fight against a blue-uniformed enemy. Above all, in each the central protagonists pursue a lengthy quest, the solution to which proves to embody their own physical form. This is perhaps more evident, infamous even, in *The Prisoner*, where McGoohan's Number Six finally unmasks his nemesis, Number One, only to discover his own face, laughing back at him in manic glee.

This final episode, premonitorily entitled 'Fallout', left UK audiences as confused and frustrated as had *Magical Mystery Tour*. For Leslie Halliwell it 'explained nothing and fell apart almost completely, the intention apparently being to make a statement about Vietnam' (1986: 499). It does, perhaps, literalise the statement attributed to Sun Tsu that 'to know your enemy you must become your enemy'. But it can also be interpreted at a more indigenous and, in line with differing national countercultural practices, personal rather than socio-political level. With self-expression hampered by the urge to conform, *The Prisoner* allegorises a perceived British – or rather English – sense of repression, revealing, as Greg Rowland notes, how the English 'excel at keeping the status quo intact, perhaps entertaining some whimsical ideas of rebellion for a short while, but in the end they will always love Big Brother' (*SF:UK*, Channel 4, March 2001). Comfortable (and sceptical) Albion again.

   Yellow Submarine adopts a similar allegorical structure but sails in the opposite direction. At the start of their final battle, the liberators from Liverpool meet their identical physical doubles in the form of Sgt. Pepper's Lonely Hearts Club Band, freed from their glass bubble to the opening clavioline strains of 'Baby, You're A Rich Man'. This musical signposting is important with the song ostensibly alluding to 'the beautiful people', the self-adopted name of the US West Coast's 'doped up' hippie community – their first British flowering at Alexandra Palace's 14-hour Technicolor Dream festival on 29th April 1967 had Lennon in attendance and is understood to have inspired his 'laid-back' song (Davies 2014: 262–3). 'Baby, You're A Rich Man' can also be read, though, as articulating 'the problems of identity, felt with devastating acuteness, even anguish, by four lads from Liverpool transported overnight on a magical mystery tour to fame, fabulous fortune and the omnipresent, all-embracing culture of the global village' – a cogent underscoring of how, in short, 'the drug theme exists because of the search for identity' (Mellers 1973: 102).

   Acting on this musical signpost, *Yellow Submarine* can ultimately be interpreted as the rich but lost Beatles engaged on a dangerous, drug-fuelled quest to 'find themselves'. Its narrative quest may begin with Ringo but its resolutionary doubling is centred on John. The character of Jeremy may originally have been sourced from *Beyond the Fringe* stalwart Jonathan Miller (Bassett 2012: 157). However, he is introduced in the film as embodying and accompanied by 'Nowhere Man', a Lennon composition with a 'Help!'-like autobiographical slant, reflecting an unsettled Beatle high on drugs, low on self-esteem, and devoid of personal or professional direction (Davies 2014: 127). Jeremy's description of himself as, amongst other things, an 'eminent physicist' equates with John the cartoon savant, while 'hard-hitting satirist' – some might adjudge 'lousy poet, too' – fits with Lennon the published author.

As such, John's initial refusal to have anything to do with Jeremy can be read as a denial of his former self – much as Jeremy's final flower-power success over the Chief Blue Meanie equates with the new self-confident, peace-conscious, Ono-loving Lennon. Beyond provenance and parallels, however, John's duality, briefly glimpsed in his Janus-faced mirror-image in the theatre corridor during *A Hard Day's Night*, is here explicitly fore-grounded in the denouement as the Fab Four-times-two confound the four-headed Bulldog. From the mechanical piano's upper panel John emerges and sings that 'You Can Talk To Me', a lyric read by MacDonald as 'rather menacingly pointed (possibly at McCartney)' (1994: 243). Here, though, less confrontationally, another panel opens to reveal as interlocutor a sec-ond John, the self-professed 'alter ego' for the egg/ego man. As the four-headed hound backs down, a finally fulfilled John, 'at one' with himself, can help to bring a similar unity to the whole of Pepperland.

If the spiritual resolution carries through, the social relevance is ulti-mately more problematic. In both *Yellow Submarine* and *The Prisoner* this 'finding of oneself' occurs in a battle scenario to the strains of 'All You Need Is Love', but the cartoon's karmic completion of self contrasts with the more ironic stance of the television series, which concludes in apocalyp-tic chaos amidst rifles and the bomb. The difference is crucial, as this ced-ing of flower power to fire power illustrates a major cultural shift between 1967 and 1968. Following police clashes with anti-Vietnam war demonstra-tors at London's Grosvenor Square on 17 March 1968, Britain's alternative counterculture lurched towards a more oppositional and Maoist New Left. Exposing the obverse of the medium's aesthetic advantage over mimesis, the two works' endings indicate how a live action series could respond to swiftly changing social currents while a painstakingly completed animated feature had to remain with previously established story lines.

The wider public clearly preferred the happy ending – the Beatles, after the faux-pas of *Magical Mystery Tour*, briefly regained their cross-generational appeal, while McGoohan was forced into hiding to escape the wrath of viewers. Alexander Walker was mistaken, though, in praising the Beatles cartoon for capturing the *zeitgeist*: in truth, it missed youth culture by a good year – and the Edwardian costumes by two years. This *was* sensed by a few contemporary critics, John Russell Taylor, for instance, noting a datedness in 'a real document of the fleeting moment at which one can already see "now" becoming "period"' (1968). By the time *Yellow Submarine* was released, it was an historical document: the Summer of Love was long past. Even in tea-loving Albion, 1968 was messy and discordant, a time more redolent of Prisoners than Pepperland. The Beatles, so long in person the vanguard of cinema and youth culture, were now, in animation, off the pace.

But not out of pocket. Pauline Kael bemoaned the transformation of 'yesterday's outlaw idols of the teenagers' into 'a quartet of Pollyannas for the wholesome family trade' (1968: 153). It was undoubtedly difficult to reconcile the countercultural message of *Yellow Submarine* with the unprecedented swell of ancillary merchandise. 'Wasn't this supposed to be what the Beatles were against?' Kael asked, perhaps forgetful of the economic imperative permeating their Richard Lester films. In partial mitigation, *Yellow Submarine* succeeded in bringing the animated film to a fresh audience – the politically committed and economically vital 18–30 youth market. In Britain access to animation had been limited to London's New Cinema Club, or the few provincial theatres bold enough to use the Short Film Service. *Yellow Submarine*, as Leslie Felperin Sharman notes, 'packaged the visual style of the avant-garde for a mass audience... It cleared a space for animation in the art houses' (1994: 15).

It was a template the Beatles themselves would look to explore further. Though they had already made a film about being pursued through exotic landscapes by a mystical cult seeking a revered ring, the Beatles next proposed a collaboration with Stanley Kubrick on a musical adaptation of JRR Tolkien's *Lord of the Rings*, a work popular with countercultural-ists, who saw in it parallels with their own struggles to be free of oppressive forces. United Artists, who deemed the Beatles' coda appearance in *Yellow Submarine* insufficient to complete their three-picture deal, had just acquired the book's film rights, but Kubrick passed on the project, citing the text's unfilmable size (Norman 2016: 324). In any case Tolkien, deeply antipathetic to pop music, refused point-blank to sanction the Beatles' participation – an unvoiced Ortonesque 'fuck them' to the prospect of John playing Gollum, Paul as Frodo, George as Gandalf and Ringo as Sam.

The Beatles' new-found love of animation would have to await later solo (parental) projects and a different literary slant. For McCartney this came notably/notoriously with Mary Tourtel's Rupert Bear comic strip character in *Rupert and the Frog Song* (Dunbar, 1984), while Ringo voiced the Reverend Wilbert Awdry's *Railway Series* books in *Thomas the Tank Engine & Friends* (UK 1984–86; US 1989–90)[7] – works more in tune with country comforts than the counterculture. Instead, to fulfil their cinema contract the Beatles eventually agreed to be filmed in their preferred working location, a process documentary in the recording studio that would (hopefully) allow the increasingly squabbling and rancorous group to 'let it be'.

Notes

1 *Little Malcolm* (Cooper, 1974) would eventually become the first feature film executive produced by George Harrison, who also supplied incidental music for the soundtrack.
2 For more details see *Heritage Auctions Catalogue* (2014).
3 MacDonald's appraisal is, in truth, more applicable to the earlier *Help!*, where McCartney later admitted that 'We showed up a bit stoned, smiled a lot and hoped we'd get through it' (Beatles 2000: 169).
4 Ringo's interest in photography is acknowledged in his solo riverside scene in *A Hard Day's Night* where he makes comic play with a Pentax 35mm camera (di Franco 1978: 13–4).
5 The 'corporation t-shirts' were not entirely acquiescent since the BBC cut a romantic scene on Tregurrian Beach featuring Aunt Jessie and Buster Bloodvessel (Ivor Cutler) kissing and cuddling to an orchestrated version of 'All My Loving'. While the Summer of Love was tolerated for the young, it was seemingly beyond the pale for older generations.
6 The independently-published *Oz* magazine (1963–73) is considered 'the leading journal' of the counterculture era (Green 1998: 356).
7 Ringo would also provide the framing narration for the home video release of Harry Nilsson's more anti-authoritarian *The Point!* (Wolf, 1971).

4   The Beatles' conclusion

Let It Be (1970) and legacy

Let It Be, the final Beatles film, offers a concise encapsulation of their earlier screen work's narrative, stylistic and thematic preoccupations while also unambiguously signalling the end of the long sixties' youth and countercultural positivity. Together with selected entries from the group's later solo ventures, it presages the move into a historicist phase for British cinema and youth culture, and therefore the concluding chapter of this volume will discuss these films both in terms of their relationship to youth cultures and more broadly in how they impacted British cinema.

Let It Be – leaving youth culture

Let It Be again had its origins in television with McCartney the catalyst, looking to unite the fractious four after the discordant recording sessions for the double *White Album*. He suggested a project where the quartet would 'get back' to their rock'n'roll roots and end the decade with a live filmed performance, monumental in scope but free from the studio intricacies that had increased their musical sophistication but undermined group solidarity. The broad concept was considered promising – a similar concert broadcast had proven successful with Bob Precht's documentary of their 15 August 1965 record-breaking *The Beatles at Shea Stadium* (BBC 1, tx. 1 March 1966, ABC, tx. 10 January 1967) – and mooted venues now progressed from the initially booked Roundhouse Theatre[1] to encompass playing in Liverpool Cathedral, a disused Thames-side flour mill, a slowly-filling Roman amphitheatre in Libya, a Native American reservation in New Mexico, even on board Cunard's cruise liner the *Queen Elizabeth*, 'singing the middle eight as the sun comes up' (Cott and Dalton 1970: 20). None met with unanimous approval (Harrison and Starr vetoed travelling abroad) but, with the venue still undecided, it was agreed to start filming studio rehearsals for an accompanying television documentary. Paul particularly warmed to the concept of a process piece, having recently seen

Henri-Georges Clouzot's recording of painterly creativity in *Le Mystère Picasso/The Mystery of Picasso* (1956).[2]

While Glyn Johns was entrusted with the sound recording, American-born baronet Michael Lindsay-Hogg, familiar to the group from his promotional films to 'Paperback Writer' and 'Rain' (May 1966), plus 'Revolution' and 'Hey Jude' (September 1968), was brought in to direct, and on 2 January 1969 the group, with no ready material, convened at Twickenham Film Studios.[3] A minimal film crew and two cameras were employed for most sessions, but the large sound stage, while appropriate for shooting much of *A Hard Day's Night* and *Help!*, was not conducive to musical creation, and a fortnight later, after arguments and a walkout from George, the group relocated to their Savile Row Apple Studio and the television documentary plus live concert concept were dropped in favour of a single feature-length 'Get Back' movie (Lewisohn 1992: 306–7). This is usually interpreted with a narrative (and legal) neatness as allowing the Beatles to fulfil their contractual commitment to United Artists. In truth, though, this deal now mattered little to the group and, in any case, would have been difficult to enforce under English law (O'Dell 2002: 79). It is far more likely that, with their new Apple Corps company haemorrhaging money, the cash-conscious quartet were appraised that a theatrical release would prove far more lucrative. Once again the economic imperative must be acknowledged.

With Ringo due to start shooting *The Magic Christian* (for Apple Films) in February, time to hone a new set of songs was short, but the addition of keyboardist Billy Preston – known since their 1962 Star Club days in Hamburg – sufficiently lifted spirits and limited internecine spats to ensure a productive fortnight and a viable album's worth of material. To bring the film project to a conclusion, an impromptu in situ performance was then agreed, leading the Beatles, on Thursday 30 January, to play their new set on the roof of their Apple Corps building: final studio recordings followed the next day. Thereafter the Beatles moved on, coming together in April 1969 to record the *Abbey Road* album but drifting further apart over the acrimonious (Paul-opposed) May appointment of Allen Klein as manager. Unhappy with/uninterested in the results of their 'Get Back' sessions, in March 1970 Harrison and Lennon (unbeknownst to McCartney or George Martin) allowed Klein to replace Johns with American producer Phil Spector to shape the audio tracks into a serviceable album. Spector proceeded to undermine the project's whole 'back-to-basics' aesthetic by over-dubbing 'The Long and Winding Road', 'Across the Universe' and 'I Me Mine' with his trademark washes of strings and choirs, further exacerbating the group's artistic differences.[4]

Lindsay-Hogg, meanwhile, had been left to edit down the 500 rolls of film, some 55 hours of footage, into an 80-minute work for theatrical release. His inclusions, while conveying some of the interpersonal ten- sions – notably George arguing with Paul over a guitar part on 'Two of Us' – followed group instructions not 'to have a lot of the dirty laundry' on show. He therefore removed from the initial 210-minute cut all ref- erences to George's walkout and reduced footage of the distracted John and Yoko Ono (Unterberger 2006: 332–3). The final film version, blown up from 16mm standard TV format to a cropped 35mm widescreen, fol- lows a broadly chronological three-act structure, equally divided between Twickenham, the Apple Studio and the rooftop concert. However, by the time Spector's remixed album was released, 16 months after the recording sessions, and Lindsay-Hogg's completed film, now pertinently retitled *Let It Be*, premiered in New York on 13 May 1970 – its UK London/Liverpool premiere followed a week later – the Beatles (as of 10 April) had split. None attended any of the film premieres.

The *Let It Be* album, while indifferently reviewed, immediately topped both US and UK charts, as did the title track single. The film *Let It Be*, despite (ironically) gaining the now-ex-Beatles their first Academy Award, for Best Original Song Score, was savaged by the critics, with mainstream hostility recalling the levels accorded to *Magical Mystery Tour*. British writer and film director Tony Palmer, for whom the Beatles had become 'the centre, the excuse for the world's focus on the cult of youth', adjudged that here they 'starred in one of the worst films ever made'. *Let It Be* was, he felt, distinctly 'amateur' and 'a bore. It's supposed to show the Beatles at work, but it doesn't. Shot without any design, clumsily edited, defeatedly titled "A Feature Film", uninformative, awkward and naïve, it would have destroyed a lesser group' (1970). Regular Beatle reviewer Felix Barker concluded that 'the film's music ought to satisfy their fans. To the less committed, this may look more like the last whimper of a dying civilisation' (1970).

Several reviewers, like Patrick Gibbs, questioned the wisdom of the whole undertaking: 'Artists are generally wise not to let the public see how the wheels go round and, in fact, the Beatles do nothing of the kind, merely going through the motions of improvisation and creation' (1970). Especially given the trailer's promise of 'a bioscopic experience' showing the group 'rapping, relaxing and philosophising', Nina Hibbin conveyed the general sense of disappointment: 'For those expecting it to throw some light on the development of the Beatles phenomenon, it is disappointingly barren' (1970). Despite the 'fly-on-the-wall' format, the Beatles yet again – frustratingly for most – seemingly escaped cinematic 'capture'. For Tom Hutchinson 'it is only incidentally that we glimpse anything about their *real* characters – the way in which music now seems to be the only unifying force holding them together; the way Paul McCartney chatters incessantly even when, it seems, none of the others is listening' (1970). Alexander

Walker, implying a replay of *Magical Mystery Tour*'s self-indulgence, noted that 'like most of us who consciously fool about for home movies they are dull and unfunny' and surmised that the film was only made to complete the three-picture deal with United Artists. 'If so, this explains why it looks like a chore. Let it pass' (1970).

Much of this opprobrium is unfair as *Let It Be* exemplifies, for the second time, a Beatles film receiving criticism for not being what it never intended to be. Much as the group's 1967 avant-garde Christmas gift had been slammed for lacking a narrative, now John Russell Taylor, echoing Tony Palmer, lamented that their *Let It Be* swansong 'might be fun if it were not so grainily photographed, so incomprehensibly recorded and, at times, so erratically synchronised' (1970). More polished comedy capers were still, apparently, preferred to a low-fi process documentary which deliberately forewent the generic staples of reportage and interview, and eschewed any orienting voice-over or narrative titles. Instead, as Bob Neaverson notes, 'the only sense of temporal progression is provided by the increasingly accomplished musicianship of the Beatles, and in that sense *Let It Be* really does "let the music do the talking"' (1997: 110).

Foregoing the youthful art influences prevalent in earlier Beatles films, it is via this 'minimalist' approach that *Let It Be* instead consciously enters into negotiation with other recent rock/pop documentaries. Bob Dylan had profoundly influenced the Beatles lyrically, especially Lennon, since the *Help!* era. Here, cinematically, despite the antithetical title, one can see parallels with the direct cinema approach of D.A. Pennebaker's grainy (and tardily released) *Don't Look Back* (1967), a film which had similarly sought to convey, with minimal directorial interference, Dylan's spring 1965 acoustic concert tour of England, and had focused on backstage interactions, the working up of new material and selections from his 9–10 May Royal Albert Hall performances (Saunders 2007: 57–83).

By contrast, *Let it Be* more openly opposes the recent pop film debut of the group consistently set up as the Beatles' dark antithesis by management and media-fuelled headlines – the Rolling Stones. In reality, the groups were close personal friends and their work progressed symbiotically. After their roundly criticised sub-*Sgt. Pepper* album *Their Satanic Majesties Request* (December 1967), the Stones regrouped and (after the Beatles passed) invited Jean-Luc Godard to film them getting back to musical basics. Their productive 4–5 June 1968 sessions at London's Olympic Studios which created 'Sympathy for the Devil' were spliced with London-set agit-prop scenes of black power and Marxist proselytizing and released as the feature film *One Plus One* aka *Sympathy for the Devil* (1968).

Ever-vigilant to their 'rival' alpha-group's releases, this was a further important motivation for the Beatles project, and the two works offer significant symbiotic connections and situational contrasts. At a practical level, influential crew cross-currents are at work: Glyn Johns is the sound engineer each time; Anthony B. Richmond, Godard's cameraman on *One Plus One*, becomes the less formally-titled Tony Richmond filming *Let It Be*. Michael Lindsay-Hogg had just, on 11 December 1968, directed *The Rolling Stones Rock and Roll Circus*, a Jagger-conceived concert show (intended for BBC airing but later shelved) that included Lennon and Ono performing with the one-off 'super group' Dirty Mac. More significantly, both films are of culturally historical importance for providing the sole extensive footage of the respective groups in (late-1960s) rehearsal and recording mode (Glynn 2013: 141–52).

Thereafter all is complete contrast. While the diptych *One Plus One* successfully offers a Clouzot-like depth in its detailed record of the creative evolution of a single song, the tripartite *Let It Be* plumps instead for breadth, squeezing in myriad numbers at differing levels of gestation with seminal tracks largely presented only in their final version. This is particularly regrettable with McCartney's driving 'Get Back' which evolved through several iterations. It started as an adjacent Caribbean 12-bar that (with Conservative MP Enoch Powell's April 1968 'rivers of blood' speech still impactful) satirised British fears of Commonwealth immigration. Later it became a country blues song with lyrics in (Reeperbahn) German and eventually evolved into the final album and single versions, offering career-summative riffs on dope-smoking and, in a return to exploring gender fluidity, transsexuality. It was also characterised by a compositional process where, according to Lennon, every time Paul sang 'Get back to where you once belonged' he looked pointedly at Yoko (MacDonald 1994: 292). To cap it all, the final edit's paucity of footage featuring key(board) player Billy Preston arguably repeats the racial displacements of *Help!*.

Similarly regrettable is the omission of all session work on 'All Things Must Pass'. This not only misses an apposite summation of the current group dynamic, but also replicates the longstanding Lennon-McCartney hierarchy that failed to recognize an increasingly frustrated Harrison's matured songwriting.[5] In short, Godard's film catches the Rolling Stones' successful reversion to origins in a burst of creative energy: Lindsay-Hogg's film of the Beatles, conversely, traces and even magnifies the drawn-out drip-feed demise of a musical collective.[6]

Despite their different trajectories both films bear witness to a shared impulse. As Philip Norman cogently notes of the Beatles, 'It was as if, to rediscover themselves as musicians, they were putting themselves through the kind of endurance test that Hamburg used to be; seeking to reactivate those old, tight sinews with music that stretched back to their creative birth' (2003: 370). However, if the austerity and rawness of *Let It Be* achieves this goal in its cinematic styling, 'getting back' proved a predominantly vain undertaking both musically and interpersonally. Positively, the group offer a raucous and happy rendition of their 1957 skiffle-blues number 'One After 909' – 'one of the first songs we'd ever done', Paul reminisces on camera. However, an early Apple Studios rock'n'roll medley is distinctly sub-standard, with John, creatively hampered by heroin, unable to recall the lyrics or structure to Smokey Robinson's 'You Really Got a Hold on Me' – an admittedly complex song but previously covered with some panache on *With the Beatles*. Even a new composition like Paul's elegiac, Everly Brothers-sounding 'Two of Us' is contaminated by current anxieties, the line 'You and me chasing paper, getting nowhere' referencing the ongoing contractual problems that would explode into litigation two days after these studio sessions ended.

Despite the constant filming, nowhere is there a moment of joy to match Paul's youthful smile straight to camera from *A Hard Day's Night*. Throughout, the audio-visual content of *Let It Be* reveals not just maturing 'serious' artists with progressively incompatible visions, but separate family men whose prime concern is no longer 'hanging out with the boys'. The dropping of an album cover recreating/updating Angus McBean's EMI stairwell photograph as featured on 1963's *Please Please Me* was judicious since the one generation not represented in this final Beatles film is the (fresh-faced and poptimistic) teenager.[7] During the Apple Studio sessions, Heather Eastman, the six-year-old daughter of Paul's partner, Linda, can be seen playing around the studio. During the smattering of applause that follows the Beatles' rooftop concert, Paul's 'thanks, Mo' addresses Ringo's wife, the watching Maureen Starkey. Even George, in his week's departure, reportedly travelled north to visit his parents, Harold and Louise.

Above and beyond these acknowledgements (and absences), the film significantly registers the constant presence at John's side of his partner since May 1968, the Japanese Fluxus artist Yoko Ono. With this volume's focus on 'the Beatles growing up' on screen across the 1960s, several factors, notably claustrophobic fan pressures and the moor-loosening loss of Brian Epstein, have been seen to contribute to their spiteful demise, and another is brought to the fore here. A summative narrative could hold that the Beatles phenomenon, while not denigrating the contributions of George and Ringo, is in essence the story of John and Paul, two Liverpool youths who meet up and become the best of friends, until drifting apart due to girlfriends and then marriage – the confirmation of adulthood. This is notably the case with the high-profile Ono, a ubiquitous and evidently alienating studio presence throughout the making of *Let It Be* (see Figure 4.1).

The group had long upheld an embargo on partners in the recording studio, but by now John was demonstrably no longer interested in the

Figure 4.1. Let It Be – not getting back to where they once belonged.

Beatle collective (thus making Paul the group's default – and occasion-ally over-demanding – decision-maker) nor in its proven working practices. Lindsay-Hogg's framing and editing regularly emphasise Yoko's pres-ence – positively in a cut to Yoko watching John's rooftop declaration of devotion in 'Don't Let Me Down', more divisively when John and Paul's (rare) enjoyment of an early duet on 'Two of Us' is undercut by a brief shot of Yoko brooding by the wall. Less manipulated is the final Twickenham scene where, as George works with Paul and Ringo on his new (and appo-sitely solipsistic) composition 'I Me Mine', an openly disdainful John eschews any expert contribution and instead waltzes around the studio with his new love.

This impromptu dance, though far removed from John's 'cool' Eddie Cantor transformation in *Yellow Submarine*, pointedly reveals John's artis-tic preoccupations and collaborations to be now fully centred on Yoko. Together they had recently made the 'Unfinished Music' sound collages 'Two Virgins' and 'Life with the Lions', while cinematically, through their new Bag Productions company, their work took John far beyond his peers' avant-garde experiments – and any youth/pop culture appeal. Positive efforts included the Super 8 super-slow-motion *Smile* aka *No. 5* (1968) and the double-exposure superimpositions of *Two Virgins* (1968). More provoc-atively, the *Peeping Tom*-like *Rape* aka *No. 6* (1969) showed a woman (Eva Majlata) being relentlessly pursued by the POV camera across London until cornered in her apartment. Commenting on how individual (and group) privacy is despoiled to entertain a viewing public, the theme potentially reworked the worst of Beatlemania but also resonated uncomfortably with the 'Get Back' sessions' documentary process.

That viewing public to be entertained would be problematised in the film's closing rooftop concert – the last public performance the Beatles would ever give. *Let It Be*'s earlier studio sessions, unlike the recording scenes featured in *Help!*, exposed a process from which the collective 'mojo' had largely disappeared, its disconnect registered (and George's walkout obscured) by the prevalence of medium shots and extreme close-ups. The live performance, however, with 16 cameras in total, several on adjacent roofs allowing a greater percentage of wide shots, suddenly showed well-grooved ensemble players offering up (in the half-length final edit) ebullient if suitably rough-and-ready versions of 'Get Back' (first and last), 'Don't Let Me Down', 'I've Got a Feeling', 'One after 909' and 'Dig a Pony'. Despite the telling absence of any Harrison composition (and Lennon needing a lyric sheet for 'Dig a Pony'), it is a joyous reaffirmation of togetherness, a reminder of how tight a live band they had been in their youth, and an adrenalised set displaying intuitive interplay and mutual respect – at one point the reputedly reluctant George even swaps exaggerated 'rock star' poses with John, who offers a genuine 'Thank you, brothers' at the end of 'Dig a Pony'.

However, after a breach of the peace was reported by a nearby bank manager – one imagines a workplace realisation of Johnson's warring commuter from *A Hard Day's Night* – the arrival of officers from Savile Row Police Station during a reprise performance of 'Get Back' reiterates the more 'staged' nature of this last act (cameras are conveniently if clandestinely ready at the Apple entrance). Coming upstairs to break up the concert, the police visually replicate the music-menacing Blue Meanies from the recent *Yellow Submarine*, agents of the Establishment still stifling (post-)counter-culture creativity – and protecting Mayfair business lunches. Structurally, though, and stylistically – with the multiple angles and repeated fore-grounding of the filming process, notably clapper loaders dodging between cameras – the performative conclusion again harks back to the group's film origins. Specifically, it is reminiscent of the Scala concert climaxing *A Hard Day's Night* where the tightly-spliced set visually validated the closing harmonised claim that 'She Loves You'.

A significant absence here, however (implicit in John's 'thank you'), is that direct connection outward with those fans and the reciprocal waves of rapture emanating from spectators such as the young 'White Rabbit', so integral to the success of the Scala sequence and, at that time, the necessary group completion. The Beatles had long tired of such mass teen hysteria. Here, though, perched at the centre of a five-storey high and windswept

rooftop (playing midday as back in their Cavern Club residency), they can-
not even be *seen* by the mixed demographic briefly filmed on the streets
below, a public whose interview answers interrupt the filmed performance
rather than unifyingly complement it. Or uniformly compliment it. One
elderly gent finds that 'they've got good quality, they sing well' and 'they're
real good people', but an elderly woman complains that 'I just can't see that
it makes sense.' Two young women find them 'fabulous' and 'fantastic',
but another modifies her opening 'I think it's great' with the more tepid 'it
livens up the office hours, anyway'.

This is not the cross- or co-generational consensus admired by Ginsberg
and animated in *Yellow Submarine*. Nor is it the final 'boy-girl' union in
a musical 'gospel of happiness' as experienced in *A Hard Day's Night*.
Instead, as Stephanie Fremaux notes, here atop 3 Savile Row 'The lack of
a physical connection severs the normal bonding rituals that make live performance an emotional and reaffirming event' (2018: 121). Gig over, it was
back to the in-fighting and the atomised *Abbey Road*. With bonds severed
within the band and out to their audience, *Let It Be*'s single intertitle, 'THE
END', signals more than just the film's conclusion. Felix Barker may have
been dismissively ironic in his review of 'a dying civilisation', but this was
undeniably 'the disintegration of the 1960s' single most influential cultural
agents' (Frontani 2007: 211). Here, indeed, with the Beatles finally aban-
doning their enforced and prolonged collegiate adolescence, was the end of
the 1960s itself, the end of a decade of youth culture's and counterculture's
optimism and goodwill.

The Beatles' film legacy

The Beatles or the Stones? Alongside their artistic cross-fertilisation, career
longevity is another point of comparison and contrast between the two
music group titans of the 1960s. While the Stones' rock and roll b(r)and has
indefatigably persisted as a stadium-touring juggernaut, lucratively feeding
on nostalgia for an idea of their originary decade, the Beatles' trusted friend,
PA and press officer Derek Taylor reported that, in the lead-up to their split,
the quartet frequently declared that 'We can't be thirty-year-old Beatles'
(1970). As shown in *Let It Be*, the Beatles, one of its shaping constituents,
had outgrown youth culture. Equally, they had outgrown the British film
industry. Their films with Richard Lester had been key components of the
Hollywood investment in British cinema, a commercially-driven chase to
depict the social and sexual freedoms promised by the dazzling blur of
'Swinging London'. It was a funding model that, by the end of the decade,
left 90 percent of British productions financially dependent on US studios
(Dickinson and Street 1985: 233). This too could not last, and Hollywood's

repeated overextension on misjudged big-budget projects such as (who knows why) a musical version of *Goodbye, Mr. Chips* (Ross, 1969), combined with America discovering its own youth-oriented film template – a profitable New Hollywood trend initiated by *Bonnie and Clyde* (Penn, 1967) and arriving fully with *Easy Rider* (Hopper, 1969) – meant that Britain was soon financially and ideologically bereft.[8]

At the end of the 'long sixties' producer Walter Shenson could only offer a bleak prognosis of Britain, its cinema and its youth culture:

> It is a low profile country now... For an American, it is impossible to make a film reflecting the British scene – there just *is* no scene today. This place no longer makes news that is of interest to the world... all that is left is a hangover.
>
> (quoted in Walker 1974: 450–1)

He could equally have been tracing the trajectory of the Beatles' films that he helped to bring into being. As Melanie Williams notes of the decade's dynamic, 'Ebullience sliding into dissipation, synergy becoming dissent: the break-up of the emblematic 1960s band seemed to speak of much wider cultural changes, including the shift in British cinema from apparent boom to undeniable bust' (2019: 93). The dream was over.

Nonetheless, the constituent members of the Beatles continued with film work through that bust period and even, in one case, helped to reverse it. If Lennon and McCartney are incontestably the musical heart of the Beatles, their solo cinematic legacy (excluding here live concert and documentary films) lies more firmly with Starr and Harrison. John Lennon briefly continued his avant-garde collaborations with Yoko Ono. The newlyweds' 'bed-ins for peace' at Amsterdam and Montreal had featured in their 1969 films *Bed Peace*, *Honeymoon* and *Self-Portrait*, the latter controversially offering a 42-minute shot of John's intermittently semi-tumescent penis. *Fly* (1970), *Up Your Legs Forever* (1970), *Clock* (1971) and *Erection* (1971) offered Warhol-esque studies in timespans, the last not another Lennon 'dick pic' but a 19-minute time-lapse video showing the 18-month rise of Kensington's International Hotel. The couple's creative film work concluded with the television film *Imagine* (1972), mainly shot in and around their home at Tittenhurst Park in Ascot to promote Lennon's *Imagine* album. This includes a sequence where Yoko repeatedly passes through a doorway, her escorts ranging from John and his pals George Harrison and Phil Spector to the apogee of Hollywood musical stardom, Fred Astaire, previously referenced but now fully subsumed into Beatle film experimentation. More poignantly, John talks on his doorstep to an obsessed fan who has taken to sleeping in their grounds. His counsel emphatically downplays the importance of youth culture: 'Don't confuse the songs with your own life … They might have relevance to your own life, but a lot of things do.' He then invites him in for tea.[9]

While Lennon broadly maintained his countercultural credibility, McCartney went mainstream. Cinematically, Paul's greatest success was arguably artistically reuniting United Artists' Beatles and Bond behemoths with his (Grammy Award-nominated) theme song for *Live and Let Die* (Hamilton, 1973), co-written with Linda McCartney and featuring a John Barry-pastiche production from George Martin. Ever-ambitious for a total film involvement (as evidenced with his devising of *Magical Mystery Tour*), McCartney never quite 'cut it' on screen, cf. his overly self-conscious solo scene dropped from *A Hard Day's Night* (Glynn 2005: 20–1). He would retreat from fictional filmmaking when the pop musical *Give My Regards to Broad Street* (Webb, 1984), his self-penned and self-referential 'day in the life of a famous rock star', played by Paul and supported by his Rupert Bear short, received another critical (and commercial) mauling. Roger Ebert, for instance, condemned it as 'about as close as you can get to a non-movie' and 'a throwback to pre-Beatles days, back when pop musicals were simple-minded and shallow, back before *A Hard Day's Night* and *Help!* seemed to create a new tradition of fresh irreverence' (1984). McCartney would only return to the screen for an avuncular cameo in *Pirates of the Caribbean: Dead Men Tell No Tales* (Renning and Sandberg, 2017), barely causing a cultural ripple as he momentarily followed the more languid Keith Richards into Jack Sparrow's grog chorus.

By contrast, after *Let It Be*, Ringo Starr built up an eclectic portfolio with beaucoups of films. His partnership with Peter Sellers in *The Magic Christian* (McGrath, 1969), a dark but undisciplined adaptation of Terry Southern's satire on capitalism, was followed by roles in the sub-Leone spaghetti western *Blindman* (Baldi, 1971) and Frank Zappa's leftfield 'fantasy opera' *200 Motels* (Palmer and Zappa, 1971). He showed an appreciation of youth culture's current direction in directing and producing (for Apple Films) *Born to Boogie* (1972), a film where concert footage of glam rock teenage heartthrob Marc Bolan/T. Rex is combined with *Magical Mystery Tour*-style fantasy vignettes, notably a 'tea party' scene shot at Tittenhurst, now Ringo's home. Reviews were indulgent for 'the best teeny-bopper entertainment since the Beatles succumbed to insecticide' (Dignam 1972).

Starr then showed his empathy for youth culture origins as teddy boy Mike, an impressive supporting actor role to David Essex's Lennon-esque ingenu in *That'll Be the Day* (Whatham, 1973), a film which, alongside its Beatles-influenced sequel *Stardust* (Apted, 1974), furthered the 'youth heritage' explorations musically adumbrated in *Let It Be* (Glynn 2013: 165–7). Roles followed as Merlin the Magician alongside Harry Nilsson's vampire in *Son of Dracula* (Francis, 1974), as Pope Pius XI opposite Roger Daltrey's fan-beset proto-rock star in *Lisztomania* (Russell, 1975) – casting resonant with Lennon's enduring 'bigger than Jesus' remark – and as film director Laslo Karolny, one of several ex-husbands to *Sgt. Pepper* cover icon Mae West in *Sextette* (Hughes, 1978). Ringo finally took the lead as hapless *homo erectus* Atouk (and met future wife Barbara Bach) in the 'prehistoric comedy' *Caveman* (Gottlieb, 1981). The film flopped and Ringo largely retired from the screen. However, he once more caught the *zeitgeist* when guesting as himself in the pop mockumentary *Popstar: Never Stop Never Stopping* (Shaffer and Taccone, 2016), an on-the-mark parody of the over-shared promotional features favoured by latter-day teen idols such as *Justin Bieber: Never Say Never* (Chu, 2011) and *One Direction: This Is Us* (Spurlock, 2013), and a stark contrast to Lester's earlier and richly opaque Beatles films.

George Harrison had been the group's most reluctant actor – though Richard Lester subsequently thought him the most accomplished (Soderbergh 1999: 48–9) – and he made few solo screen appearances, most notably (and self-deprecatingly) his cameo as a probing television interviewer in the spoof Beatles biopic *The Rutles: All You Need Is Cash* (Idle and Weis, 1978). Behind the camera, though, his role makes him unquestionably the most important film Beatle. His close relationship with Ravi Shankar, the subject of Apple Films' documentary *Raga* (Worth, 1971), led to George headlining the pioneering and Live Aid-influencing fundraiser for famine-stricken Bangladesh: its film version, *The Concert for Bangladesh* (Swimmer, 1972), was co-produced by Harrison. Though little came of his first executive production, finally realising the David Halliwell-scripted *Little Malcolm* (1974), four years later, and principally to help his friend Eric Idle complete the troubled production of *Monty Python's Life of Brian* (Jones, 1979), George, with business manager Denis O'Brien, set up the independent film company HandMade Films. He thus secured a work redolent of both *A Hard Day's Night* and *Help!* since 'Their form of humour was in many ways anticipatory of the Pythons' (Landy 2005: 18).

George's momentary (uncredited) role in the film, part of a crowd awaiting the new Messiah, allowed him a dialectic perspective on fan idolatry. The film's international success led to him operating as executive producer on 22 further features for HandMade, a significant role that, as Ian Inglis notes, 'helped to sustain British cinema at a time of crisis, producing some of the country's most memorable movies of the 1980s' (2010: xvi). Thus George became the film facilitator that Apple Films never quite achieved. As shown in the affectionate documentary *An Accidental Studio* (Jones, Leggett and Timlett, 2019), George had the cultural and commercial capital to greenlight any project that took his fancy, get prime acting talent on board and attract outside investors. Thus valued film fare as varied as *The Long*

Good Friday (Mackenzie, 1980), *Scrubbers* (Zetterling, 1982), *A Private Function* (Mowbray, 1984), *Mona Lisa* (Jordan, 1986) and *Track 29* (Roeg, 1988) principally exist due to Harrison's involvement. He even indulged in cameos as a nightclub singer in the disastrous Madonna vehicle *Shanghai Surprise* (Goddard, 1986) and a cleaner in the anonymous *Checking Out* (Leland, 1989), before such films' late losses led to HandMade ceasing operations in 1991, and Harrison suing O'Brien for fraud and negligence before dying of lung cancer on 29 November 2001.

Notes

1 A competition in *Beatles Book Monthly* (64, November 1968) even promised tickets to the show for '50 pairs of Beatle people'.

2 Early in the recording outtakes, Paul can be heard explaining to George: 'It's like Picasso painting, where you start from nothing – coz we've started from nothing – and it'll end up as a TV show.'

3 On Brian Epstein's insistence on a 'visually bland', quasi-perfunctory approach to the Beatles' early bespoke recordings for television, and their role in establishing the 'pop promo' format, see Smith (2019: 530–2).

4 The album as originally envisaged – at least by McCartney who tried unsuccessfully to block Spector's version – was released as *Let It Be...Naked* in November 2003.

5 Harrison's newly prolific creativity would burst out in *All Things Must Pass*, his rapturously received solo triple album released in November 1970. Richard Williams thought it 'the rock equivalent of the shock felt by pre-war moviegoers when Garbo first opened her mouth in a talkie: Garbo talks! – Harrison is free!' (1970).

6 At the time of writing it was announced that Peter Jackson, fresh from *They Shall Not Grow Old* (2018), had signed on to make a similarly digitised (and more upbeat) documentary version of *Let It Be* from the existent in-studio footage (Aswad 2019).

7 McBean's photographic recreation finally appeared in 1973 as the cover of the retrospective *The Beatles/1967–70* aka *The Blue Album*.

8 The Beatles' influence on New Hollywood? Ian MacDonald sees *Magical Mystery Tour* 'as a prototype of ... the "road movie" genre inaugurated two years later by *Easy Rider*' (1994: 224).

9 Lennon has monopolised the solo Beatle biopic. His early years are treated in *In His Life: The John Lennon Story* (Carson, 2000) and the BAFTA-nominated *Nowhere Boy* (Taylor-Wood, 2009). His late-Beatle life and beyond is the focus of *John and Yoko: A Love Story* (Stern, 1985) and *Lennon Naked* (Coulthard, 2010). A legendary 1976 visit from Paul to the Dakota is recreated in *Two Of Us* (Lindsay-Hogg, 2000), while an alternative history, where Lennon left the Beatles in 1962, is poignantly recounted in *Snodgrass* (Blair, 2013).

Epilogue

And in the end? Patrick Cargill's superintendent from the 'Metropolitan scuffers' in *Help!* may have spoken for many at the time when asking the Beatles 'How long do you think you'll last?', but last they have, ever-popular and influential down the generations. The Beatles' musical legacy is incontrovertible, but beyond their variable solo ventures the quartet have also remained a significant presence in (fictional) film culture, especially its 'youth heritage' narratives. For instance, Beatlemania narratives drive both *I Wanna Hold Your Hand* (Zemeckis, 1978), set at Ed Sullivan's CBS Studio 50 (and the first executive-producer credit for Steven Spielberg), and its antipodean variant *Secrets* aka *One Crazy Night* (Pattinson, 1992), a coming-of-age tale set around the Fab Four's June 1964 arrival in Melbourne. References to their cultural import can be found in myriad movies and various contexts, from *Almost Famous* (Crowe, 2000) where the veteran groupie is called Penny Lane (Kate Hudson), through to *Sister Act* (Ardolino, 1992) where convent-dwelling Deloris Wilson (Whoopie Goldberg) lists Jesus' disciples as John, Paul, George and Ringo (without ensuing Mid-west record burnings). The Beatles' songbook shapes 'structures of feeling' in youth-centred films ranging from the jukebox musical *Across the Universe* (Taymor, 2007) with its 1960s star-crossed lovers, to the rom-com mystery of *Yesterday* (Boyle, 2019), two films with rooftop concerts in the style of *Let It Be*.

Above all, though, the five films that the Beatles made together and released between 1964 and 1970 signify both synchronically and diachronically, with their musical numbers and narrative arcs serving to chart a seminal decade's development of youth culture when the Beatles were the acknowledged 'mission control'. Beginning with the celebration of Britain's own 'youthquake' in the joyous and genre-shifting *A Hard Day's Night*, the Beatles' film work allows us to examine their indicative musical maturation and coded retreat from the tribulations of stardom in *Help!*, their tentative attempts at improvised filmed 'happenings' in the televised

Magical Mystery Tour, their acceptance of cartoon representations as leaders of the hippie counterculture in *Yellow Submarine*, and the final (lightly expurgated) implosion of their musical dynamic in the recording studios of *Let It Be*.

Condensing further their films' indicative importance, if a single example were sought to encapsulate the Beatles' socio-cultural impact, a prime candidate would have to be their encounter in *A Hard Day's Night* with Johnson, the pompous commuter whose generational disagreeableness leads him to order the Fab Four to leave his first-class carriage for 'some other part of the train where you so obviously belong'. The Beatles pointedly did not go where others/elders thought they obviously belonged. Instead they retorted with a confident and confounding humour, asserting their rights to equal status and asking the curmudgeon for a kiss. Nor did they stay in their allotted place in wider society where their success worked to pull a nation out of mourning, erode barriers of class and age and even, as Jon Wiener notes, 'helped loosen the straitjacket of conventional sex roles' (1991: 47). Nor did they keep to their station in the film world where their ambition shifted the pop music film's genre codes and conventions, led them to move across media and bring a countercultural agenda into a nation's living-rooms and movie screens, and synthesised current rock documentary techniques to record their own 'swan song'. Throughout their career the Beatles reinforced the excellence of their music with the power of their personalities and the infectiousness of their irreverence. It was a combination that formed a key motor of the youth culture and counterculture that they projected on film and that endures therein for our education and entertainment. As John replied to Scotland Yard's dismissive superintendent, 'Can't say fairer than that!'

Bibliography

'A Hard Day's Hunt' (1967) *Daily Mirror*, 12 April, p. n/a.

'*A Hard Day's Night* Review' (1964) *Monthly Film Bulletin,* Vol. 31, No. 367, p. 121.

Alpert, H. (1965) '*Help!* Review,' *Saturday Review*, 28 August, p. n/a.

Altman, R. (1987) *The American Film Musical*, Indiana: Indiana University Press.

Ansen, D. (1978) 'Stigwood's Home Movie,' *Newsweek*, 31 July, p. 42.

Arena: Magical Mystery Tour Revisited (Hanly, 2012, BBC Four, 6 October, 55 min).

Aronowich, A.G. (1964) 'Yeah! Yeah! Yeah! Music's Gold Bugs: The Beatles,' *Saturday Evening Post*, 21 March, pp. 30–5.

Aswad, J. (2019) 'Jackson's Forthcoming Beatles Film Shows *Let It Be* Sessions Were Actually Rather Jolly,' *Variety*, 30 January, p. n/a.

'Bad Trip' (1968) *Time*, 22 November, p. 80.

Barker, F. (1964) 'At Last – I Scream for the Beatles,' *Evening News*, 9 July, p. n/a.

Barker, F. (1965) 'I'd Like to Help the Beatles,' *Evening News*, 29 July, p. n/a.

Barker, F. (1968) 'Beatles, Meanies and Stark Raving Bonkers!' *Evening News*, 18 July, p. n/a.

Barker, F. (1970) '*Let It Be* Review,' *Evening News*, 22 May, p. n/a.

Bassett, K. (2012) *In Two Minds: A Biography of Jonathan Miller*, London: Oberon Books.

BBC News (1999) 'Best 100 British Films – Full List,' online, 23 September, http://news.bbc.co.uk/1/hi/entertainment/455170.stm.

Bean, R. (1964) 'Keeping up with the Beatles,' *Films and Filming*, Vol. 15, No. 5, February, pp. 9–12.

Beatles, The (2000) *The Beatles Anthology*, London: Cassell.

Biskind, P. (1998) *Easy Riders, Raging Bulls: How the Sex 'N' Drugs 'N' Rock 'N' Roll Generation Saved Hollywood*, London: Bloomsbury.

Bourne, S. (1996) *Brief Encounters: Lesbians and Gays in British Cinema 1930–1971*, London: Cassell.

Bowman, D. (1972) 'Scenarios for the Revolution in Pepperland,' *Journal of Popular Film*, Vol. 1, No. 3, Summer, pp. 173–84.

Braun, M. (1964) *Love Me Do! The Beatles' Progress*, Harmondsworth: Penguin.

Brown, N. (2017) *British Children's Cinema: From the Thief of Bagdad to Wallace and Gromit*, London: I.B. Tauris.

Brown, P. and Gaines, S. (1984) *The Love You Make: An Insider's Story of the Beatles*, London: Pan.

Buskin, R. (1994) *Beatle Crazy! Memories and Memorabilia*, London: Salamander Press.

Carr, R. (1996) *Beatles At the Movies: Scenes from a Career*, London: Harper Collins.

Catterall, A. and Wells, S. (2001) *Your Face Here: British Cult Movies Since the Sixties*, London: Fourth Estate.

'Chase & Superchase' (1965) *Time*, 3 September, p. 84.

Clarke, J., Hall, S., Jefferson, T. and Roberts, B. (1976) 'Subcultures, Cultures and Class: A Theoretical Overview,' in S. Hall and T. Jefferson (eds) *Resistance Through Rituals*, London: Hutchinson, pp. 9–74.

Clayson, A. (2003) *Ringo Starr*, London: Sanctuary.

Cleave, M. (1966) 'How Does a Beatle Live? John Lennon Lives Like This,' *Evening Standard*, 4 March, p. 10.

Cohn, N. (1969) *AwopBopALooBop AWopBamBoom: Pop from the Beginning*, London: Weidenfeld and Nicolson.

Coleman, J. (1965) 'Advertisements for the Beatles,' *New Statesman*, 30 July, p. n/a.

Coleman, J. (1968) '*Yellow Submarine* Review,' *New Statesman*, 28 July, p. n/a.

Coleman, R. (1963) 'On Tour with THEM!' *Melody Maker*, 9 November, p. 9.

Connolly, R. (1981) *John Lennon 1940–1980*, London: Fontana.

Corliss, R. and Schickel, R. (2005) 'All-*Time* 100 Movies,' *Time*, 12 February, p. n/a.

Coryton, D. and Murrells, J. (1990) *Hits of the 60s: The Million Sellers*, London: B.T. Batsford.

Cott, J. and Dalton, D. (1970) 'Daddy Has Gone Away Now,' *Rolling Stone*, 9 July, p. n/a.

Cowie, P. (1989) *Coppola*, London: Andre Deutsch.

Creasy, M. (2011) *Beatlemania! The Real Story of the Beatles UK Tours 1963–1965*, London: Omnibus Press.

Crowther, B. (1964) 'The Four Beatles in *A Hard Day's Night*,' *New York Times*, 12 August, p. 41.

Crowther, B. (1965) 'Beatles Star in *Help*! Film of the Absurd,' *New York Times*, 24 August, p. 25.

Davies, H. (2014) *The Beatles Lyrics: The Unseen Story Behind Their Music*, London: Weidenfeld and Nicolson.

Davies, H. (2016) *The Beatles Book*, London: Ebury Press.

de Kloet, J. and van Zoonen, L. (2007) 'Fan Culture – Performing Difference,' in E. Devereux (ed) *Media Studies: Key Issues and Debates*, London: Sage, pp. 322–41.

Denisoff, R.G. and Romanowski, W.D. (1991) *Risky Business: Rock in Film*, New Brunswick, NJ: Transaction.

Dewhurst, K. (1967) 'The Beatles' *Magical Mystery Tour*: A Romantical View of Show Business,' *Guardian*, 28 December, p. n/a.

di Franco, J.P. (1978) *The Beatles in Richard Lester's A Hard Day's Night – A Complete Pictorial Record of the Movie*, Harmondsworth: Penguin.

Dickinson, M. and Street, S. (1985) *Cinema and State: The Film Industry and the British Government, 1927–84*, London: British Film Institute.

Dignam, V. (1972) '*Born to Boogie* Review,' *Morning Star*, 20 December, p. n/a.

Drummond, N. (1968) 'I Still Say Beatles' *Tour* Was Entertaining,' *New Musical Express*, 6 January, p. 3.

Dyer, R. (1992) *Only Entertainment*, London: Routledge.

Ebert, R. (1984) '*Give My Regards to Broad Street* Review,' *Chicago Sun-Times*, 24 October, p. n/a.

Ehrenreich, B., Hess, E. and Jacobs G. (1992) 'Beatlemania: Girls Just Want to Have Fun,' in L.A. Lewis (ed) *The Adoring Audience: Fan Culture and Popular Media*, London: Routledge, pp. 84–106.

Evans, M. (1984) *The Art of the Beatles*, London: Anthony Blond.

Ewens, H. (2019) *Fangirls: Scenes from Modern Music Culture*, London: Quadrille.

Felperin Sharman, L. (1994) 'Animatophilia,' *Sight and Sound*, Vol. 4, No. 7, 'Art into Film' Supplement, July, pp. 14–16.

Fremaux, S. (2018) *The Beatles on Screen: From Pop Stars to Musicians*, New York: Bloomsbury.

French, P. (1965) 'Richard Lester,' *Movie*, No. 14, Autumn, pp. 5–11.

Frontani, M. (2007) *The Beatles: Image and the Media*, Jackson: University of Mississippi Press.

Gelmis, J. (1971) *The Film Director As Superstar*, London: Secker and Warburg.

Gibbs, P. (1965) 'No Knack with the Beatles,' *Daily Telegraph*, 30 July, p. n/a.

Gibbs, P. (1968) 'Beatles Find Their Film Feet in Weird and Witty Fantasy,' *Daily Telegraph*, 17 July, p. n/a.

Gibbs, P. (1970) '*Let It Be* Review,' *Daily Telegraph*, 22 May, p. n/a.

Gillett, C. (1983) *The Sound of the City*, revised edition, London: Souvenir Press.

Gilliatt, P. (1964) 'Beatles in Their Own Right,' *Observer*, 12 July, p. n/a.

Gladwell, M. (2008) *Outliers: The Story of Success*, London: Allen Lane.

Gledhill, C. (1991) 'Signs of Melodrama,' in C. Gledhill (ed) *Stardom: The Industry of Desire*, London: Routledge, pp. 207–29.

Glynn, S. (2005) *A Hard Day's Night*, London: I.B. Tauris.

Glynn, S. (2008) 'From Pepperland to *The Prisoner*: *Yellow Submarine* and Social Change,' in J. Helbig and S. Warner (eds) *Summer of Love: The Beatles, Art and Culture in the Sixties*, Trier: WVT, pp. 147–60.

Glynn, S. (2011) 'The Beatles' *Help!*: Pop Art and the Perils of Parody,' *Journal of British Cinema and Television*, Vol. 8, No. 1, pp. 23–43.

Glynn, S. (2013) *The British Pop Music Film: The Beatles and Beyond*, London: Palgrave Macmillan.

Glynn, S. (2016) *The British School Film: From Tom Brown to Harry Potter*, London: Palgrave Macmillan.

Gosling, N. (1968) 'Lessons at the Movies,' *Observer*, 28 July, p. n/a.

Gould, J. (2007) *Can't Buy Me Love: The Beatles, Britain and America*, London: Piatkus.

Graham-Dixon, A. (1996) *A History of British Art*, London: BBC.

Gray, A. (1964) '*A Hard Day's Night* Review,' *New Musical Express*, 10 July, p. 3.

Green, J. (1967) '*Magical Mystery Tour* Review,' *Evening News*, 27 December, p. n/a.

Green, J. (1998) *All Dressed Up: The Sixties and the Counterculture*, London: Jonathan Cape.

Greene, D. (2008) *Politics and the American Television Comedy*, Jefferson, NC: McFarland & Company.

Gregg, R. (2017) 'Sanitizing the Beatles for Revolution: Music, Film and Fashion in the 1960s and *A Hard Day's Night*,' in E. Paulicelli, D. Stutesman and L. Wallenberg (eds) *Film, Fashion, and the 1960s*, Bloomington: Indiana University Press, pp. 17–33.

Halliwell, L. (1986) *Halliwell's Television Companion*, third edition, London: Grafton.

Hanke, K. (1989) 'The British Invasion of the 1960s: Part II,' *Films in Review*, Vol. 40, No. 5, May, pp. 269–77.

Harcourt, P. (1965) '*Help!* Review,' *Sight and Sound*, Vol. 34, No. 4, Autumn, p. 199.

Harris, J. (2012) 'Fab Furore,' *Guardian*, 25 September, p. n/a.

Harry, B. (1984) *Beatlemania: An Illustrated Filmography*, New York: Avon.

Harry, B. (1992) *The Ultimate Beatles Encyclopedia*, London: Virgin.

Heritage Auctions Catalogue (2014) Dallas, Texas, 4–6 December.

Hewitt, P. (2011) *Fab Gear: The Beatles and Fashion*, New York: Prestel.

Hibbin, N. (1965) 'Never a Pause for Breath,' *Daily Worker*, 31 July, p. n/a.

Hibbin, N. (1968) 'Beatles Bring a New Film Dimension,' *Morning Star*, 17 July, p. n/a.

Hibbin, N. (1970) '*Let It Be* Review,' *Morning Star*, 23 May, p. n/a.

Hieronimus, R. (2002) *Inside the Yellow Submarine*, Iola: Krause.

Hinxman, M. (1968) '*Yellow Submarine* Review,' *Sunday Telegraph*, 21 July, p. n/a.

Hoggart, R. (1957) *The Uses of Literacy: Aspects of Working-Class Life*, London: Chatto and Windus.

Houston, P. (1965) 'Commercials à la Mode,' *Financial Times*, 30 July, p. n/a.

Hughes, R. (1991) *The Shock of The New*, second edition, London: Thames and Hudson.

Hutchins, C. (1965) '*Help!* Review,' *New Musical Express*, 30 July, p. n/a.

Hutchinson, T. (1970) '*Let It Be* Review,' *Sunday Telegraph*, 24 May, p. n/a.

Ingham, C. (2006) *The Rough Guide to the Beatles*, second edition, London: Rough Guides.

Inglis, I. (2008) 'Cover Story: Magic, Myth and Music,' in O. Julien (ed) *Sgt. Pepper and the Beatles: It Was Forty Years Ago Today*, Bristol: Ashgate, pp. 91–102.

Inglis, I. (2010) *The Words and Music of George Harrison*, Santa Barbara: Praeger.

Inglis, I. (2012) *The Beatles in Hamburg*, London: Reaktion.

Inglis, I. (2013) 'The Beatles,' Oxford Bibliographies, online, https://www.oxfordbi bliographies.com/view/document/obo-9780199757824/obo-9780199757824 -0085.xml.

James, D.E. (2016) *Rock 'N' Film: Cinema's Dance with Popular Music*, Oxford: Oxford University Press.

Jenour, K. (1967) 'Beatles' Mystery Tour Baffles Viewers,' *Daily Mirror*, p. 1.

Johnson, P. (1964) 'The Menace of Beatlism,' *New Statesman*, 28 February, pp. 326–7.

Joseph, P. (1973) *Good Times: An Oral History of America in the Nineteen Sixties*, New York: Charterhouse.

Kael, P. (1968) 'Metamorphosis of the Beatles,' *New Yorker*, 30 November, p. 153.

Kael, P. (1994) *For Keeps: 30 Years at the Movies*, New York: E.P. Dutton.

Lahr, J. (ed) (1986) *The Orton Diaries*, London: Methuen.

Landy, M. (2005) *Monty Python's Flying Circus*, Detroit: Wayne State University Press.

Lang, D. (2009) 'Six Boys, Six Beatles: The Formative Years, 1950–1962,' in K. Womack (ed) *The Cambridge Companion to the Beatles*, Cambridge: Cambridge University Press, pp. 9–32.

Leech, K. (1976) *Youthquake: Spirituality and the Growth of a Counter-Culture*, London: Sphere.

Lefcowitz, E. (1989) *The Monkees Tale*, Berkeley, CA: Last Gasp.

Lewis, J. (1992) *The Road to Romance and Ruin: Teen Films and Youth Culture*, London: Routledge.

Lewisohn, M. (1992) *The Complete Beatles Chronicle*, London: Hamlyn.

Lewisohn, M. (2013) *The Beatles: All These Years: Tune In*, London: Little, Brown.

Livingstone, M. (2000) *Pop Art: A Continuing History*, second edition, London: Thames and Hudson.

Lowey, I. and Prince, S. (2014) *The Graphic Art of the Underground: A Countercultural History*, London and New York: Bloomsbury.

MacDonald, I. (1994) *Revolution in the Head: The Beatles' Records and the Sixties*, London: Fourth Estate.

Mailer, N. (1969) *The Armies of the Night: History As a Novel/The Novel As History*, New York: Signet.

Malone, M. (1967) 'No Magic in this Sad Beatles' Tour,' *Daily Mirror*, 27 December, p. n/a.

Marlborough, D. (1967) '*Magical Mystery Tour* Review,' *Daily Mail*, 27 December, p. n/a.

Marwick, A. (1996) *British Society Since 1945*, third edition, London: Penguin.

Marwick, A. (1998) *The Sixties: Cultural Revolution in Britain, France, Italy and the United States c.1958–1974*, Oxford: Oxford University Press.

Mathijs, E. and Sexton, J. (2011) *Cult Cinema*, Oxford: Wiley-Blackwell.

McElhaney, J. (2009) *Albert Maysles*, Urbana: University of Illinois Press.

McKinney, D. (2003) *Magic Circles: The Beatles in Dream and History*, Cambridge, MA: Harvard University Press.

McRobbie, A. (1980) 'Settling Accounts with Subcultures: A Feminist Critique,' *Screen Education*, No. 34, pp. 111–23.

Mellers, W. (1973) *Twilight of the Gods: The Beatles in Retrospect*, London: Faber and Faber.

Melly, G. (1972) *Revolt into Style*, Harmondsworth: Penguin.

Merritt, D. (1987) *Television Graphics: From Pencil to Pixel*, London: Trefoil Publications.

Miles, B. (1997) *Paul McCartney: Many Years from Now*, London: Secker & Warburg.

Mundy, J. (1999) *Popular Music on Screen: From Hollywood Musical to Musical Video*, Manchester: Manchester University Press.

Nathan, D. (1968) 'Nice Trip in a Sub Until the Beatles Sink,' *Sun*, 17 July, p. n/a.

Neaverson, B. (1997) *The Beatles Movies*, London: Cassell.

Neaverson, B. (2000) 'Tell Me What You See: The Influence and Impact of the Beatles' Movies,' in I. Inglis (ed) *The Beatles, Popular Music and Society: A Thousand Voices*, London: Macmillan, pp. 150–62.

Norman, P. (2003) *Shout! The True Story of the Beatles*, revised edition, London: Sidgwick & Jackson.

Norman, P. (2008) *John Lennon: The Life*, London: HarperCollins.

Norman, P. (2016) *Paul McCartney: The Biography*, London: Weidenfeld and Nicolson.

Nott, J. (2015) *Going to the Palais: A Social and Cultural History of Dancing and Dance Halls in Britain, 1918–1960*, Oxford: Oxford University Press.

Nowell-Smith, G. (1964) '*A Hard Day's Night* Review,' *Sight and Sound*, Vol. 33, No. 4, Autumn, pp. 196–7.

O'Brien, D. (2000) *SF:UK: How British Science Fiction Changed the World*, London: Reynolds & Hearn.

O'Dell, D. (2002) *At the Apple's Core: The Beatles from the Inside*, London: Peter Owen.

Orwell, G. (1998 [1948]) *Nineteen Eighty-Four*, London: Penguin.

Palmer, T. (1970) 'The Beatles' *Let It Be* Is a Bore. Thank Heavens for the Music,' *Observer*, 24 May, p. n/a.

Paulicelli, E. and Wallenberg, L. (2017) 'Introduction,' in E. Paulicelli, D. Stutesman and L. Wallenberg (eds) *Film, Fashion, and the 1960s*, Bloomington: Indiana University Press, pp. 1–14.

Perkins, R. and Stollery, M. (2004) *British Film Editors: The Heart of the Movie*, London: British Film Institute.

Pieper, J. and Path, V. (2005) *The Beatles Film & TV Chronicle 1961–1970*, Stockholm: Premium Publishing.

Pines, J. (2008) 'British Cinema and Black Representation,' in R. Murphy (ed) *The British Cinema Book*, third edition, London: British Film Institute, pp. 118–24.

Powell, D. (1968) '*Yellow Submarine* Review,' *Sunday Times*, 21 July, p. n/a.

Quigly, I. (1964) 'The Beatles: *A Hard Day's Night*,' *Spectator*, 10 July, p. n/a.

Ray, R.B. (1985) *A Certain Tendency of the Hollywood Cinema, 1930–1980*, Princeton, NJ: Princeton University Press.

Raynor, H. (1967) 'Beatles Anarchic Mystery,' *Times*, 27 December, p. n/a.

Reiter, R. (2008) *The Beatles on Film: Analysis of Movies, Documentaries, Spoofs and Cartoons*, Bielefeld: Transcript.

Richards, D. (1968) 'Beatles Magic Shines Through Cartoon Frolic,' *Daily Mirror*, 17 July, p. n/a.

Richards, J. and Aldgate, A. (1983) *British Cinema and Society 1930–1970*, Oxford: Basil Blackwell.

Riley, T. (1988) *Tell Me Why*, London: Bodley Head.

Robinson, D. (1968) '*Yellow Submarine* Review,' *Financial Times*, 19 July, p. n/a.

Sarris, A. (1964) 'Bravo Beatles!' *Village Voice*, 27 August, p. 13.

Saunders, D. (2007) *Direct Cinema: Observational Documentary and the Politics of the Sixties*, London: Wallflower.

Savage, J. (2015) *1966: The Year the Decade Exploded*, London: Faber and Faber.

Scott-Jones, A. (1964) '*A Hard Day's Night* Review,' *Daily Mail*, 16 July, p. n/a.

Shanes, E. (2009) *Pop Art*, New York: Parkstone.

Shillinglaw, A. (1999) '"Give Us a Kiss": Queer Codes, Male Partnering and the Beatles,' in P.J. Smith (ed) *The Queer Sixties*, New York: Routledge, pp. 127–44.

Sinyard, N. (2010) *The Films of Richard Lester*, Manchester: Manchester University Press.

Smith, J. (2019) 'Absence and Presence: *Top of the Pops* and the Demand for Music Videos in the 1960s,' *Journal of British Cinema and Television*, Vol. 16, No. 4, pp. 492–544.

Soderbergh, S. (1999) *Getting Away with It*, London: Faber and Faber.

Stanley, B. (2013) *Yeah Yeah Yeah: The Story of Modern Pop*, London: Faber and Faber.

Stark, S.D. (2005) *Meet the Beatles: A Cultural History of the Band That Shook Youth, Gender and the World*, New York: Harper Collins.

Sutton, D. (2000) *A Chorus of Raspberries: British Film Comedy 1929–1939*, Exeter: University of Exeter Press.

Taylor, D. (1970) 'The Beatles Split: A Report from a Front-row Seat,' *Chicago Tribune*, 26 July, p. n/a.

Taylor, D. (1987) *It Was Twenty Years Ago Today*, London: Bantam Press.

Taylor, J.R. (1968) 'A British Colour Film That Will Please Nearly Everyone,' *Times*, 18 July, p. n/a.

Taylor, J.R. (1970) '*Let It Be* Review,' *Times*, 22 May, p. n/a.

Thomas, J. (1967) 'Magic Leaves Beatles with Mighty Flop,' *Daily Express*, 27 December, p. n/a.

Thornton, M. (1964) 'What a Triumph This Is for Those Beatles,' *Sunday Express*, 13 July, p. n/a.

Thornton, M. (1965) 'That Old Beatle Magic Is Beginning to Wane,' *Sunday Express*, 1 August, p. n/a.

Turner, R. (1967) 'Even Beethoven Wasn't Great All the Time,' *Daily Express*, 28 December, p. n/a.

Unterberger, R. (2006) *The Unreleased Beatles: Music and Film*, San Francisco: Backbeat.

Various (1964) *The New Generation: 1964*, exhibition catalogue, London: Whitechapel Gallery.

Walker, A. (1965) 'The Beatles Strike Out on a Limb,' *Evening Standard*, 27 July, p. n/a.

Walker, A. (1968) 'A Mod-Odyssey,' *Evening Standard*, 18 July, p. n/a.

Walker, A. (1970) '*Let It Be* Review,' *Evening Standard*, 21 May, p. n/a.

Walker, A. (1974) *Hollywood, England: The British Film Industry in the Sixties*, London: Michael Joseph.

Walker, A., Taylor, S. and Ruchti, U. (1999) *Stanley Kubrick, Director*, London: Weidenfeld and Nicholson.

Wenner, J. (1973) *Lennon Remembers: The Rolling Stone Interviews*, Harmondsworth: Penguin.

Wheen, F. (1982) *The Sixties*, London: Century Publishing.

Whitcombe, I. (1972) *After the Ball: Pop Music from Rag to Rock*, Harmondsworth: Penguin.

Whiteley, N. (1987) *Pop Design: Modernism to Mod - Theory and Design in Britain 1955–1972*, London: Design Council.

Wiener, J. (1991) *Come Together: John Lennon in His Time*, Chicago: University of Illinois Press.

Williams, M. (2019) 'The 1950s and 1960s,' in J. Hill (ed) *A Companion to British and Irish Cinema*, Hoboken, NJ: Wiley-Blackwell, pp. 84–105.

Williams, R. (1970) '*All Things Must Pass* Review,' *Melody Maker*, 28 November, p. n/a.

Williams, R. (2005 [1980]) *Culture and Materialism*, London: Verso.

Wilson, C. (1964) 'Merseybeat Marxes!' *Daily Mail*, 7 July, p. n/a.

Wolfe, T. (1989 [1968]) *The Electric Kool-Aid Acid Test*, London: Black Swan.

Womack, K. (2010) '"Nothing's Going to Change My World": Narrating Memory and Selfhood with the Beatles,' *Style*, Vol. 44, Nos. 1–2, Summer/Spring, pp. 261–81.

'Yeah? Yeah, Yeah!' (1964) *Time*, 14 August, p. 67.

Yule, A. (1994) *The Man Who "Framed" the Beatles: A Biography of Richard Lester*, New York: Donald I. Fine Inc.

Index